BONJOUR Emily

BONJOUR *Emily*

An Unofficial Cookbook for Fans of *Emily in Paris*

DAHLIA CLEARWATER

Skyhorse Publishing

Copyright © 2023 by Hollan Publishing

Skyhorse Publishing books may be purchased in bulk at special discounts for sales promotion, corporate gifts, fund-raising, or educational purposes. Special editions can also be created to specifications. For details, contact the Special Sales Department, Skyhorse Publishing, 307 West 36th Street, 11th Floor, New York, NY 10018 or info@skyhorsepublishing.com.

Skyhorse® and Skyhorse Publishing® are registered trademarks of Skyhorse Publishing, Inc., a Delaware corporation.

Visit our website at www.skyhorsepublishing.com.

10 9 8 7 6 5 4 3 2 1

Library of Congress Cataloging-in-Publication Data is available on file.

Photos used by permission of Shutterstock.com

Print ISBN: 978-1-5107-7528-2
eBook ISBN: 978-1-5107-7776-7

Printed in China

CONTENTS

♥

BIENVENUE . . . TO PARIS!

WELCOME TO EMILY'S CITY OF LIGHTS, where *ringarde* fashion, unrelenting optimism, and the pleasures of French cuisine are just a flight of stairs or a designer-scooter ride away. Some call it "cringe," but let's call it "binge." It's the enthusiasm, pep, and indulgent perspective of *Emily in Paris* that checks off that wanderlust box and sends every rom-com lover's heart fluttering.

Bonjour Emily is a delightful and tantalizing food tour of some of the show's most mouthwatering moments—from the tension-filled preparation of the GTC Omelet (page 33) and the groan-worthy first bite of #Je T'aime, Paris, Pain au Chocolat (page 4) to the Five Star Burrata & Heirloom Tomato Salad (page 38) and the Affair of Legends Lamb Shanks (page 80). Feeling nostalgic for that Chicago hospitality? There's Chicago Deep Dish Pizza (page 76) and Skokie, IL, USA Funfetti Cupcakes (page 97) to remind you of home. No culinary adventure is complete without a toast, so *santé* with an Exclusive Lavender Martini (page 120) or belly up to a British pub and walk out with a man on one arm and The Traveler (page 130) in the other hand.

This pretty-in-Paris cookbook will have you feeling the *joie de vivre* of Emily Cooper with each bite. Complete with fun food for wandering cobblestone streets, small bites befitting an influencer lunch, sexy mains prepared by the hottest chef in France (or at least Normandy), sweet treats from every boulangerie, and zesty-yet-sophisticated cocktails—this book will transport you to Parisian heaven.

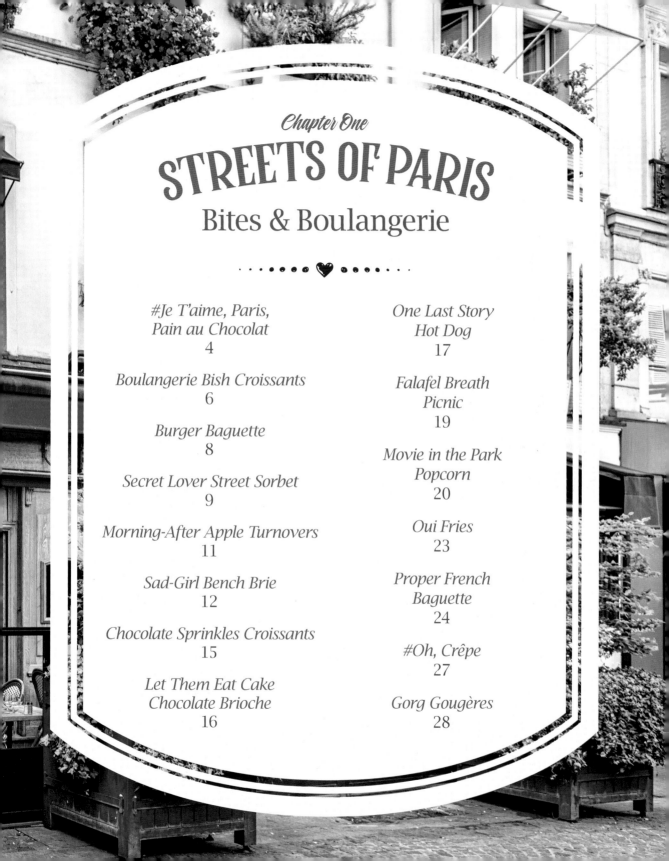

Chapter One

STREETS OF PARIS

Bites & Boulangerie

· · · · · ● ● ● ● 🖤 ● ● ● ● · · ·

#JE T'AIME, PARIS, PAIN AU CHOCOLAT

· · · · ● ● ● ● ♥ ● ● ● · · · · ·

Is it un pain *or* une pain? *Fire up that social media and take your first sumptuous bite of these buttery, chocolatey, and altogether heavenly pastries. This recipe is simplified for ease (leave the painstaking dough-making to the French) but is full of flavor and nostalgia for that first pâtisserie love. Enjoy #Je T'aime, Paris, Pain au Chocolat on a sunny morning.*

Makes 12 pastries
· · · · · · · · · · · · · · · · ·

All-butter croissant dough

All-purpose flour, for dusting

24 (3-inch) chocolate batons

2 teaspoons whole milk

1 large egg

2 cups hot water

1. Prepare 2 baking sheets with parchment paper.

2. Place refrigerated croissant dough onto a lightly floured surface and sprinkle some flour on top. Roll the dough into a 19 × 11-inch rectangle. Trim the edges of the dough down to an 18 × 10-inch rectangle and discard the leftover dough. Then cut the dough down to 12 rectangles, about 5 × 3 inches each.

3. Transfer the rectangles onto 1 lined baking sheet without overlapping the dough. Cover the baking sheet tightly with plastic wrap and refrigerate for 15 minutes.

4. Remove the baking sheet from the refrigerator and lay out the dough on a clean work surface. To form the pain au chocolat, place 1 chocolate baton on the first rectangle of dough crosswise about ½ inch from the edge of the bottom. Place another chocolate baton about 1½ inches from the top of the rectangle. From the bottom, begin rolling the dough up all the way to the top, allowing the first chocolate baton to roll over the second chocolate baton so they sit next to one another in the dough like opera glasses (with a layer of dough dividing them). Press the seam to secure.

5. Repeat this process to make 12 pastries. Place each pain au chocolat seam-side down onto the lined baking sheets about 2 inches apart.

6. In a small bowl, whisk the milk and the egg to make an egg wash. Brush the pastries with half of the egg wash and then save it in the refrigerator for later.

7. Transfer the baking sheets to a cold oven. Place an oven-safe bowl of the hot water in the oven with the pastries, shut the door, and let proof for 1 to 2 hours or until the pastries have doubled in size. Remove the baking sheets from the oven and let stand for 30 minutes.

8. Preheat the oven to 425°F. Apply a second coat of egg wash to the pastries on 1 baking sheet and place on the middle rack of the oven. Reduce the oven temperature to 375°F right away and bake for 18 to 24 minutes, or until golden brown. Repeat this process with the second sheet of pastries. Serve warm.

BOULANGERIE BISH CROISSANTS

· · · · ● ● ◗ ♥ ◖ ● ● ● · · ·

You could go to your local boulangerie to get a warm buttered pastry worthy of a social post, or you could indulge in these Boulangerie Bish Croissants. This process isn't for the faint of heart, but the results may just sweep you off your feet.

Makes 8 croissants
· · · · · · · · · · · · · · · · ·

FOR THE PASTRIES

¼ cup unsalted butter, cut into ½-inch blocks

4⅔ cups all-purpose flour, plus more for dusting

1 tablespoon plus ½ teaspoon kosher salt

¼ cup granulated sugar

2¼ teaspoons active dry yeast

1½ cups whole milk, at room temperature

FOR THE BUTTER LAYER

1½ cups unsalted butter

2 tablespoons all-purpose flour

1 large egg

2 tablespoons heavy cream

1. In the bowl of a stand mixer fitted with the dough hook attachment, mix together the butter, flour, salt, sugar, and yeast. Mix on a low speed for about 1 minute, and then stream in the milk. Increase the speed to medium and mix until the dough separates from the sides of the bowl.

2. Remove the dough from the bowl and work it into a ball with floured hands. Score the top of the dough with a plus sign, return the ball to the mixing bowl, and cover with plastic wrap. Let the dough rise at a warm room temperature for about 45 minutes or until it is 1½ times its size. Transfer the dough to the refrigerator to chill for at least 4 hours or overnight.

3. For the butter layer, beat the butter and flour with a hand-mixer until it is smooth. Transfer the butter to a baking mat and smooth it out to a 7 × 10-inch rectangle with precise edges. Chill the butter layer in the refrigerator for 30 minutes.

4. On a lightly floured work surface, roll out the dough. Place the butter layer in the center of the dough and fold the dough edges over it, using your fingers to seal the edges. Roll the dough on a lightly floured work surface until it is a 10 × 20-inch rectangle. Fold the dough into thirds like a letter. Roll the dough out a second time to another 10 × 20-inch rectangle. Fold the dough into thirds like a letter for a second time. On a parchment-lined baking sheet, transfer the dough to the refrigerator, covered, to cool for 30 minutes.

5. Roll the dough out a third time to another 10 × 20-inch rectangle. Fold the dough into thirds like a letter for a third time. On a parchment-lined baking sheet, return the dough to the refrigerator, covered, to rest for 1 hour.

6. Remove the dough from the refrigerator and place it onto a lightly floured work surface to rest for 5 minutes. Roll it out to a 14 × 17-inch rectangle. Brush off excess flour and wrap the dough in plastic wrap and return it to the baking sheet. Freeze the slab for 20 minutes and then refrigerate it for at least 8 hours.

7. Unwrap the dough and place it onto a lightly floured work surface and dust off any excess flour. Use a pizza cutter to cut an inch off the rectangle so that it's 16 inches long, then slice into four 4 × 14-inch strips. Separate the strips and slice each of them diagonally to form 8 triangles. Slice the short side of each triangle a tiny bit so that the triangle sides are of equal length.

8. Very gently, stretch out the dough triangles to be 3 inches wider and slightly longer than when you started. Roll up the triangles into crescent shapes and place them on two parchment-lined baking sheets with the end of the dough strips face-down. Let the croissants rest at room temperature for 1 hour, then transfer to the refrigerator to cool for 1 to 12 hours.

9. Preheat the oven to 375°F.

10. To make an egg wash, whisk together the egg and the heavy cream. Brush onto the croissants.

11. Bake the croissants in the oven for 20 minutes on both racks. Rotate the baking sheets and swap oven racks. Bake for another 10 minutes or until golden brown. Remove the croissants from the oven and allow to cool on a wire rack. Serve warm.

BURGER BAGUETTE

· · · · ● ● ● ♥ ● ● ● · · ·

Even dreamy chefs from Normandy crave fast food. This American-in-size and French-in-flavor burger will satisfy your hunger without all the romantic heartache.

Makes 1 burger
· · · · · · · · · · · · · · · ·

1 baguette

2 burger patties

2 slices Emmental cheese

1 leaf romaine lettuce

1 tablespoon Dijon mustard

1. Slice the baguette lengthwise and lightly toast, cut-side down.

2. Cook the patties on a grill or grooved skillet on medium-high heat for 4 minutes. Flip the patties and grill for another 4 minutes or until desired temperature.

3. Top with the cheese for the last minute of cooking and cover to allow the cheese to melt.

4. Remove the patties from the heat and place them on the bottom half of the baguette. Place the romaine on top.

5. Spread the mustard on the inside of the top half of the baguette and top the sandwich.

SECRET LOVER STREET SORBET

·········· ♥ ··········

Nothing brings out Sylvie's sweet tooth like a paramour. This super-quick sorbet will satisfy your strawberry cravings and won't embarrass you when you bump into your ex.

Makes 2 cones
·················
3 cups frozen strawberries

2 tablespoons honey

2 waffle cones

1. In the bowl of a food processor or blender, blend the strawberries until smooth. If the strawberries get stuck, add a little bit of warm water and use a spatula to scrape the sides.

2. Taste the sorbet and blend in the honey as desired to reach your preferred sweetness.

3. Scoop the sorbet into waffle cones or transfer to a freezer-safe container to firm up before serving.

MORNING-AFTER APPLE TURNOVERS

*There is only one reason Sylvie brings pastries to the office,
and it's a good one. To everyone's glee, these Morning-After Apple
Turnovers make an appearance when she's feeling extra generous.*

Makes 4 pastries

4 medium apples, peeled
and chopped

2 tablespoons butter

2 teaspoons cornstarch

1 teaspoon ground cinnamon

½ cup packed brown sugar

1 sheet puff pastry

1 large egg

1 teaspoon water

1 tablespoon turbinado sugar

1. Preheat the oven to 400°F. Prepare a baking sheet with parchment paper.

2. In a large saucepan over medium-high heat, bring the apples, butter, cornstarch, cinnamon, and brown sugar to a boil. Reduce the heat and simmer for about 5 minutes or until the mixture has thickened and the apples are fork tender.

3. On a lightly floured work surface, roll out the puff pastry into a 15-inch square. Cut the pastry into 4 squares.

4. Spoon the apple mixture onto the center of each pastry square. Fold the pastries over diagonally to form triangles, or "turnovers." Press the seams of the dough to seal the pastries.

5. In a small bowl, whisk the egg and the water to make an egg wash.

6. Transfer the pastries to the lined baking sheets. Brush with the egg wash and sprinkle them with the turbinado sugar.

7. Bake the turnovers for 25 to 30 minutes or until golden brown.

SAD-GIRL BENCH BRIE

· · · · • • ● ♥ ● • • · · · ·

Not all French cuisine needs to be complex and confusing like a brooding neighborhood chef. This simple Sad-Girl Bench Brie is happier than it sounds and even easier to prepare. Just grab a few ingredients from your local fromagerie and enjoy it on a park bench or shrouded in blankets on your couch. You may even make a new ex-pat BFF in the process.

Makes 2 servings

· · · · · · · · · · · · · · · ·

1 (8-ounce) Brie round

¼ cup toasted walnuts, roughly chopped

2 sprigs fresh thyme

Honey, for drizzling

Wine, for drinking

1 fresh baguette, for serving

1. Assemble the Brie and walnuts on a cheese board. Place the thyme on the board for decoration, or remove the leaves from the stems and sprinkle them atop the cheese. Drizzle the Brie with honey, or serve it on the side so your guest can incorporate it as needed.

2. Serve the cheese board with wine and a roughly torn fresh baguette, or slice and toast the bread so the Brie gently warms with each bite.

CHOCOLATE SPRINKLES CROISSANTS

· · · · • • ● ● ♥ ● ● • • · · · ·

Chocolate Sprinkles Croissants are the love-child of the boulangerie's pain au chocolat and warm, buttery croissants. These easy-to-make and easier-to-eat pastries will taste like you just grabbed them on your way home from your French class.

Makes 12 pastries
· · · · · · · · · · · · · · · ·

All-butter croissant dough

12 squares dark chocolate

All-purpose flour, for dusting

2 teaspoons whole milk

1 large egg

¼ cup chocolate sprinkles

2 cups hot water

1. Prepare 2 baking sheets with parchment paper.

2. On a lightly floured work surface, roll out the croissant dough. If it does not already come with seams, slice the dough into 6 even strips with a pizza cutter. Slice each strip in half diagonally to form a total of 12 triangles.

3. Place the chocolate squares at the base of each triangle. Starting from the base, roll up the triangles into crescent shapes. Place them on the parchment-lined baking sheets with the end of the dough strips face-down. Cover the baking sheet tightly with plastic wrap and refrigerate for 15 minutes.

4. Remove the baking sheet from the refrigerator. In a small bowl, whisk the milk and the egg to make an egg wash. Brush the pastries with half of the egg wash and then save it in the refrigerator for later.

5. Transfer the baking sheets to a cold oven. Place an oven-safe bowl of hot water in the oven with the pastries, shut the door, and let proof for 1 to 2 hours or until the pastries have doubled in size. Remove the baking sheets from the oven and let stand for 30 minutes.

6. Preheat the oven to 425°F. Apply a second coat of egg wash to the pastries on 1 baking sheet and sprinkle them with half of the sprinkles. Place the sheet on the middle oven rack and immediately reduce the oven temperature to 375°F. Bake for 18 to 24 minutes, or until golden brown. Repeat the process with the second sheet of pastries. Serve warm.

LET THEM EAT CAKE CHOCOLATE BRIOCHE

They say that revenge is best served cold, but Emily serves it to her coworkers warm, full of chocolate chips, and in a very specific shape. It's this nervy prank that finally wins over the employees of Savoir to the power-clashing American. Shape the brioche however you like.

Makes 18 rolls

½ cup water

½ cup milk

4 tablespoons unsalted butter

3¾ cups all-purpose flour

3 eggs

3 tablespoons sugar

1½ teaspoons salt

2¼ teaspoons instant or active dry yeast

1½ cups chocolate chips

2 teaspoons whole milk

1 large egg

1. Prepare a baking sheet with parchment paper.

2. Microwave the water, milk, and butter together on low for 45 seconds or until just melted together.

3. In the bowl of a stand mixer fitted with the dough hook attachment, mix together the flour, eggs, sugar, salt, and yeast on medium speed. Stream in the milk and butter mixture. When the dough is smooth but still a little sticky, reduce the speed to low and add in the chocolate chips until evenly mixed.

4. Transfer the dough to a greased bowl, cover the dough, and let rise for 1 hour at room temperature or until doubled in size.

5. Turn the bowl over onto a clean work surface and divide the dough into 18 pieces. With lightly greased hands, roll the dough into balls and place them all on the parchment-lined baking sheet.

6. In a small bowl, whisk the milk and the egg to make an egg wash. Brush the rolls with the egg wash.

7. Preheat the oven to 400°F.

8. Cover the baking sheet with greased plastic wrap and let the dough rise at a warm room temperature for 45 minutes.

9. On the center rack, bake the rolls for 15 minutes or until golden brown.

ONE LAST STORY HOT DOG

· · · · · · ● ● ● ♥ ● ● ● · · · · ·

Turn that sad-girl frown upside down. Go out on the town with your bestie for your best montage and then prep these delicious, no-fuss hot dogs for the ultimate feast. What goes best with street-style hot dogs when you're having a bad day? Carousels and drinking champagne straight from the bottle, of course.

Makes 2 hot dogs
· · · · · · · · · · · · · · · ·

2 hot dogs

2 hot dog buns

2 tablespoons ketchup

2 tablespoons Dijon mustard

2 tablespoons green relish

2 glasses Taittinger brut champagne

1. Cut three slashes across the hot dogs. Sear the hot dogs on a grill or in a skillet on medium heat, turning every minute or so.

2. Remove the hot dogs from the heat when they are plump, browned on all sides, and the slashes have opened.

3. Place the hot dogs in the buns and top them with ketchup, mustard, and green relish. Serve with champagne.

FALAFEL BREATH PICNIC

. . . . . . ● ● ◉ ♥ ◉ ● ● . . . . .

Love is in the air, and so is busking! Turn a friendship into a dreamy, duet-inspiring romance in the park with a Falafel Breath Picnic. The hardest part is waiting for the beans and chickpeas to soak, but these wraps are as easy to compose as Benoît and Mindy's love song.

Makes 2 wraps
. . . .

FOR THE FALAFEL

1 cup dried split broad beans

½ cup dried chickpeas

2 sprigs parsley

½ yellow onion, peeled and roughly chopped

1 clove garlic

1 teaspoon cumin

1 teaspoon ground black pepper

1 teaspoon ground coriander

1 pinch cayenne pepper

1 teaspoon kosher salt

1 tablespoon baking powder

Sunflower oil, for frying

FOR THE WRAPS

2 large wheat wraps

1 Persian cucumber, julienned

2 tablespoons pomegranate arils

1 handful greens

4 tablespoons beet hummus

1. Wash the broad beans and the chickpeas and soak overnight. Drain and rinse before using.

2. In a blender, combine the chickpeas, beans, parsley, onion, garlic, spices, and baking powder.

3. Fill a saucepan with about 3 inches of sunflower oil. Heat the oil until it is shimmering. Form the falafel dough into 12 balls and gently place them in the hot oil using metal tongs or a slotted frying spoon, being careful not to splash. Turn the falafels over after 3 or 4 minutes and continue to fry another 2 to 3 minutes or until golden brown. Remove them from the oil and place them on a paper-towel-lined plate to cool and remove excess oil.

4. Lay out the 2 wraps. Divide the falafel balls, cucumber, pomegranate arils, and greens between the wraps. Add dollops of beet hummus to each wrap.

5. Roll up the wraps by folding the bottom up first to create a seal and then folding in the sides.

MOVIE IN THE PARK POPCORN

············· ♥ ·············

*Cozy up to a rom-com with this easy caramel popcorn. Share it with all
your new friends while you watch Matthew McConaughey and Kate Hudson
fall in love, or you can keep it all to yourself and your French neighbor.*

Makes 4 servings
·················

1 bag of plain popcorn

1 teaspoon kosher salt,
   plus more as desired

1 cup unsalted butter

1 cup light brown sugar

2 teaspoons vanilla extract

½ teaspoon baking soda

1. Make the bag of popcorn. Lightly salt it and toss the bag to incorporate. Pour the popcorn into a bowl and set aside.

2. In a medium saucepan, melt the butter over medium heat. Add the brown sugar and stir continuously. Bring the mixture to a boil and stir for 4 minutes. Add the vanilla, stir, and continue heating for 1 minute more. Stir in the baking soda before removing the caramel from the heat.

3. Drizzle the caramel over the popcorn and fold until the caramel covers the popcorn evenly.

4. Prepare a baking sheet with parchment paper. Spread the caramel popcorn over the baking sheet and let the caramel cool and harden before serving.

OUI FRIES

The perfect union of American and French desires: Oui Fries. These tasty potato wedges are easy to make but still offer sophistication with the aromatic rosemary. This recipe is the perfect partner for the Steak Frites (page 78).

Makes 4 servings

2 pounds Russet potatoes

3 tablespoons extra-virgin olive oil

2 tablespoons lemon juice

4 cloves garlic, minced

2 tablespoons fresh chopped rosemary

2 teaspoons dried thyme

½ teaspoon kosher salt

1. Preheat the oven to 450°F. Prepare a baking sheet with parchment paper.

2. Wash the potatoes and slice them into wedges.

3. In a large mixing bowl, combine the olive oil, lemon juice, garlic, rosemary, thyme, and salt. Toss in the potatoes to coat.

4. Spread the potatoes out evenly on the parchment-lined baking sheet.

5. Bake the potato wedges for 20 minutes and then flip them with a spatula. Bake for another 10 to 15 minutes or until crisp and golden brown.

PROPER FRENCH BAGUETTE

Is there anything better than fresh French bread? Probably not. Get the perfect crisp to these loaves with the special ice cube trick, and you'll be Paris-ready.

Makes 2 baguettes

2 tablespoons honey

1½ tablespoons active dry yeast

1½ cups warm water, divided

3½ cups all-purpose flour, plus more for dusting

2 teaspoons kosher salt

Vegetable oil, for greasing bowl

Cornmeal, for dusting pan

3 to 4 ice cubes

1. Combine the honey, yeast, and ½ cup warm water. Let the mixture rest until it begins to foam, about 5 minutes.

2. In the bowl of a stand mixer fitted with the dough hook attachment, mix together the flour and the salt on low. Slowly incorporate the yeast mixture, and then stream in 1 cup of warm water. Increase the speed to medium and mix until the dough separates from the sides of the bowl.

3. Remove the dough from the bowl and work it into a ball with floured hands for 2 to 6 minutes or until springy. Place the dough in a lightly greased mixing bowl and cover with plastic wrap. Let the dough rise at a warm room temperature until it has doubled in size, about 30 minutes.

4. On a lightly floured work surface, punch the dough down and slice it in half. To form the dough into baguettes, first make a flat rectangle out of each section. Fold the top and bottom of each section of dough to the halfway point of the rectangle and press the seams to close. Stretch the dough and then repeat the folding, sealing, and stretching process until the dough is about 12 inches long and 2 inches wide. Fold the ends to make rounded corners.

5. Dust a baking sheet with cornmeal. Transfer the baguettes to the baking sheet and lightly score them diagonally with a knife three times each. Cover the baguettes with a dish cloth and let rise until they have doubled in size, about 30 minutes.

6. Preheat the oven to 450°F. Place an oven-safe bowl or pan on the bottom rack of the oven. Transfer the baking sheet to the middle rack of the oven and toss the ice cubes into the bowl on the bottom rack at the same time. Close the oven door quickly to prevent the steam from escaping. Bake the baguettes for about 15 minutes or until golden brown.

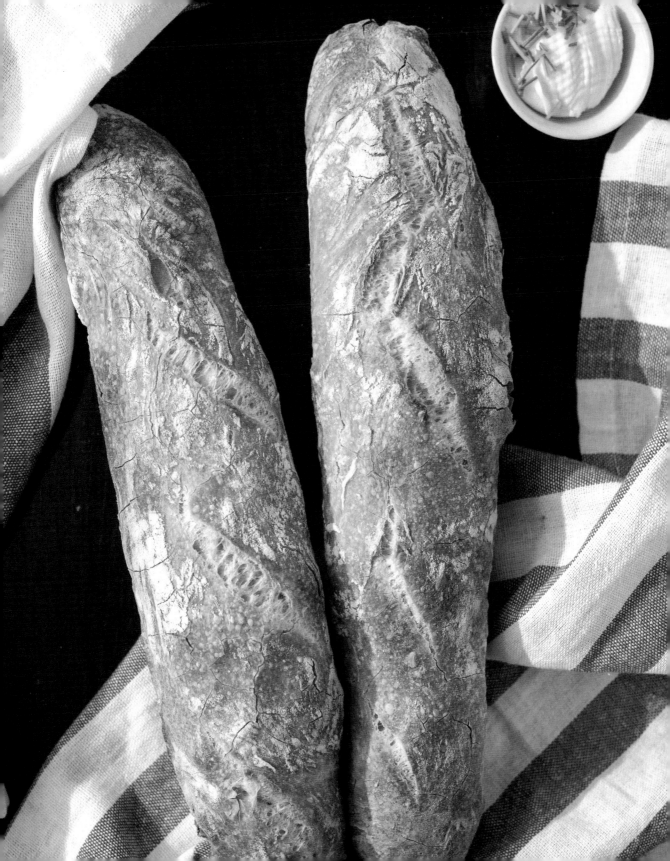

#OH, CRÊPE

· · · · ● ● ● ♥ ● ● ● · · ·

Clever hashtags are Emily's specialty. Instead of paying Parisian prices for brunch, prepare these delicious crêpes at home and come up with your own sassy sayings.

Makes 6 crêpes
· · · · · · · · · · · · · · · · ·

FOR THE CRÊPES

1 cup all-purpose flour

⅛ teaspoon kosher salt

2 large eggs

1⅓ cups nonfat milk

2 tablespoons unsalted butter, melted

FOR THE FILLING

1 tablespoon unsalted butter, divided

6 slices ham

6 ounces shredded Gruyère cheese

6 large eggs

Kosher salt, to taste

1 tablespoon fresh chives

Freshly ground black pepper, to taste

1 handful arugula

½ cup cherry tomatoes, quartered

1. In a blender, combine the flour, salt, eggs, milk, and butter. Blend until smooth and pour the mixture into a bowl. Cover and then let sit for 30 minutes.

2. Heat ½ tablespoon of the butter in a skillet over medium heat. Stir the crêpe batter and then ladle ⅓ cup of batter into the skillet. Swirl the batter in the skillet to coat. Cook for 1 minute or until the batter starts to dry out on top. Flip the crêpe with a spatula and cook for another 15 to 30 seconds or until golden brown. Remove from the pan and set aside. Repeat with the remaining batter.

3. Heat ½ tablespoon of the butter in the same skillet over medium heat and return 1 crepe to the pan. Layer 1 slice of ham and 1 ounce of cheese in the center. Crack 1 egg on top, sprinkle with salt, and fold the four sides of the crêpe inward to form a square.

4. Cover the pan and cook about 3 minutes or until the egg has reached your desired consistency.

5. Remove the crêpe from the pan. Repeat with the remaining crepes and ingredients. Garnish the finished crêpes with chives and a few turns of freshly ground black pepper. Plate with the arugula and tomatoes for added pops of color.

GORG GOUGÈRES

· · · · · ● ● ● ♥ ● ● ● · · · ·

Cheese puffs? More like Gorg Gougères. These fancy indulgences are warm, cheesy, airy, and irresistible. Elevate your snack style and pop more than a few.

Makes 24 pastries

· · · · · · · · · · · · · · · · ·

½ cup water

½ cup milk

1 stick (8 tablespoons) unsalted butter, cut into pieces

1 tablespoon sugar

1 teaspoon salt

1 cup all-purpose flour

3–4 large eggs

1 cup grated cheddar cheese

½ cup grated Gruyère cheese

1. Preheat the oven to 425°F. Prepare 2 baking sheets with parchment paper.

2. In a saucepan over low heat, combine the water, milk, butter, sugar, and salt until the butter is melted. Increase the heat to a simmer and then remove the saucepan from the heat.

3. Add the flour and stir with a wooden spoon until the mixture thickens and is free of clumps. Return the saucepan to the heat and cook, stirring, until there is a film at the bottom of the pan. Do not scrape the film off the bottom.

4. Transfer the mixture to a food processor and mix for a minute. Crack in 3 eggs one at a time and mix after each egg to make a smooth and shiny consistency. You may need to add an additional egg to achieve the right consistency. Add the cheeses and blend until mixed.

5. Scoop small balls of the mixture onto the parchment-lined baking sheets, leaving the balls 1 inch apart.

6. Place the baking sheets in the oven and reduce the heat to 375°F. Bake for 20 to 25 minutes, or until the puffs are lightly golden brown.

Chapter Two

AMUSE–BOUCHES,

Bites & Affair Starters

· · · · • • ● ♥ ● • • · · · ·

GTC OMELET

The GTC Omelet is a classic French preparation just the way Gabriel likes it.
Your cast iron pan doesn't need to bear your initials to make a great dish,
but he's right that a properly seasoned pan is what elevates this omelet's flavor.

Makes 2 omelets

4 large eggs

½ teaspoon herbes de
  Provence

Sea salt, to taste

Freshly ground black pepper,
  to taste

2 tablespoons unsalted butter,
  divided

2 handfuls microgreens

1. Whisk together the eggs, herbs, salt, and pepper until beaten.

2. In an 8-inch cast iron or nonstick pan, melt 1 tablespoon of butter over medium heat and swirl the pan to coat.

3. When the butter has melted, pour in half of the egg mixture.

4. With a rubber spatula, stir the liquid egg rapidly and shake the pan simultaneously until the egg is creamy and very lightly scrambled.

5. Remove the pan from the heat for 1 minute to rest.

6. Return the pan to medium heat and begin to roll the omelet with the rubber spatula, one quarter at a time. Turn the omelet onto a plate dressed with greens.

7. Repeat with the second omelet.

INFLUENCER LUNCH CANAPÉS

Fire up your hashtags and enjoy these delectable Influencer Lunch Canapés. Classic bites for all things elegant, these smoked salmon and cream cheese snacks have big stage presence without being hard to make. Consider springing for the large grab bags for all your guests, not just the influencers with huge followings!

Makes 12 canapés

. . . .

6 ounces cream cheese

2 tablespoons plain Greek yogurt

3 tablespoons chopped fresh chives

12 rye crackers

6 ounces smoked salmon

Kosher salt and fresh ground pepper

2–3 sprigs fresh dill, torn

1. In a medium bowl, blend the cream cheese and yogurt until smooth. Fold in the chives.

2. Prepare a serving tray with the crackers and scoop a dollop of the cream cheese mixture onto each.

3. Slice the salmon into long strips, roll them into rose shapes, and place them on the crackers.

4. Garnish with the dill.

LE CHEF HOT ASPARAGUS & JAMBON DE BAYONNE

The tiny treats in this recipe are both sophisticated and simple. You will always find asparagus in Gabriel's kitchen, and quail eggs can be found at farm stands and local grocers alike, but they transform this snack into something that will wow (all) your love interests.

Makes 8 portions

8–12 quail eggs

1 bunch asparagus, trimmed

8 slices French baguette

1 tablespoon extra-virgin olive oil

8 slices jambon de Bayonne (French prosciutto)

½ teaspoon pecorino cheese

1 pinch sea salt

1. In a medium saucepan, bring water to a boil. Gently add the quail eggs with a slotted spoon. Boil for 2½ to 3 minutes and drain the water. Cover the eggs with cold water until they are cool enough to handle. Peel the shells, slice the eggs in half, and set aside.

2. Fill the bottom half of a steam set with 2 cups of water and bring it to a boil. Place the trimmed asparagus in the top half of the steamer, cover, and steam for 5 to 7 minutes until the asparagus is cooked but still snaps. Drain the asparagus and set aside.

3. Lightly toast the baguette slices and then drizzle them with the olive oil. Top the baguette first with 1 slice of prosciutto each, several asparagus spears, and 2 to 3 halves of the quail eggs.

4. Sprinkle with the pecorino cheese and pinch of salt.

FIVE STAR BURRATA & HEIRLOOM TOMATO SALAD

· · • • ◦ ◦ ♥ ◦ ◦ • • · ·

*You don't need to fantasize about Michelin restaurants to luxuriate
in the amazing burrata salad that Emily and Gabriel share.
This salad is low effort, high reward, and it won't leave you in longing.*

Makes 2 servings
· · · · · · · · · · · · · · · · ·

6–10 small heirloom tomatoes,
   halved or quartered

1 tablespoon extra-virgin
   olive oil

2 tablespoons aged balsamic
   vinegar

Kosher salt, to taste

Freshly ground black pepper,
   to taste

1 (8-ounce) ball fresh burrata

6 leaves fresh basil

1. In a medium bowl, toss the tomatoes, olive oil, balsamic vinegar, salt, and pepper to coat.

2. Place the burrata at the center of a salad plate, slicing the top to allow the ball to open gently. Arrange the tomato mixture around the burrata and finish with the basil.

L'ESPRIT DE GIGI FISH SOUP

· · · · · ● ● ◉ ♥ ◉ ● ● · · · ·

We may never know the secret to Gigi's special fish soup or her touch in the kitchen,
but L'Esprit de Gigi Fish soup will come close. Choose a firm white fish like cod,
halibut, or sea bass for a hearty stew, and add spinach if you like greens.

Makes 4 servings
· · · · · · · · · · · · · · · · ·

6 tablespoons extra-virgin
   olive oil

1 medium yellow onion,
   peeled and chopped

4 cloves garlic, minced

⅔ cup fresh chopped parsley
   leaves

2 teaspoons tomato paste

1 (14-ounce) can crushed
   tomatoes

1 (8-ounce) bottle clam juice

½ cup dry white wine

1½ pounds firm white fish,
   cut into 2-inch pieces

1 (15-ounce) can cannellini
   beans, rinsed and drained

Several dashes Tabasco,
   to taste

1 (9-ounce) bag fresh spinach,
   optional

Kosher salt and freshly ground
   pepper

1. In a large pot over medium heat, heat the olive oil. When the oil is shimmering, sauté the onion for 3 to 4 minutes. Stir in the garlic and cook until aromatic, about 1 minute. Fold in the parsley, and then add the tomato paste and crushed tomatoes. Cook for 10 minutes, stirring often.

2. Add the clam juice, white wine, fish, and cannellini beans to the pot and bring it to a simmer. Cook until the fish is opaque, about 3 to 5 minutes. Stir in the Tabasco, salt, and pepper. Stir in the spinach until it wilts, if desired, and ladle into bowls.

HOUSEWARMING SAUCISSON EN CROÛTE

· · · • ● ● ♥ ● ● ● · · ·

Okay, so they're really just pigs in a blanket. But doesn't it sound très chic when it's in French? Tasty Housewarming Saucisson en Croûte appetizers made an appearance at Alfie's party, and Emily went into hostess mode with a full tray of them.

Makes 24 pastries
· · · · · · · · · · · · · · · ·

1 sheet puff pastry

1 egg, beaten

2 tablespoons all-purpose flour

24 cocktail sausages

1. Preheat the oven to 400°F. Prepare a baking sheet with parchment paper.

2. On a lightly floured work surface, unfold the puff pastry. Roll the pastry into a 10 × 14-inch rectangle.

3. Using a pizza cutter, slice 24 rectangles. Place the cocktail sausages at the edge of each pastry and roll to enclose, pinching the seams with your fingers. Place the pastries on the baking sheet, seam-side down, and bake for 15 minutes, or until golden brown.

GOOD LUCK, BISH SCALLOP CEVICHE

· · · • • ● ♥ ● • • · · ·

Your boss may be waiting for you to fail, but this dish is waiting to wow. The best part about ceviche is that it can be whipped up at the last minute by your heartthrob neighbor. Good Luck, Bish Scallop Ceviche includes spicy pepper paste for that unspoken heat.

Makes 4 servings
· · · · · · · · · · · · · · · · ·

½ cup fresh orange juice

½ cup fresh lime juice

1 tablespoon yellow hot pepper paste

1½ teaspoons kosher salt

½ teaspoon black pepper

¼ cup finely chopped red onion

½ pound cleaned calamari rings

½ pound sea scallops, quartered

1 (8-ounce) can corn, rinsed and drained

¼ cup chopped cilantro, optional

Zest of 1 lime

1 lime, sliced into wedges

1. To make the marinade, whisk together the orange juice, lime juice, hot pepper paste, salt, pepper, and red onion in a large bowl.

2. Chop most of the calamari rings into small chunks, leaving some rings whole for presentation.

3. In a pot of lightly simmering water, poach the calamari and scallops for 1 minute. Drain the pot and pat the scallops and calamari dry. Transfer to the bowl with the marinade. Add the corn and mix everything to coat. For the best flavor, transfer the bowl to the refrigerator, uncovered, for 3 hours, but the seafood is fully cooked when it is opaque and no longer has a pearlescent sheen.

4. Remove the bowl from the refrigerator and fold in the cilantro, if desired. Serve out portions in clean scallop shells or in large ramekins. Sprinkle with the lime zest and serve with lime wedges.

ASPARAGUS VELOUTÉ

· · · ● ● ● ♥ ● ● ● ● · · ·

It's not every man who will drop everything to impress all your bosses, clients, and magazine writers at a moment's notice, but one chef certainly can. Gabriel serves a chilled amuse-bouche to prove Emily to be l'Américaine exceptionelle.

Makes 4 servings
· · · · · · · · · · · · · · · ·

2 tablespoons extra-virgin olive oil

1 medium white onion, thinly sliced

1 pound asparagus, trimmed and cut into ½-inch pieces

½ teaspoon kosher salt

¼ teaspoon black pepper

2 cups vegetable stock

4 ounces fresh baby spinach

2–3 sprigs fresh dill, torn

1. In a large saucepan, heat the olive oil over medium heat. When the oil is shimmering, sauté the onions until they are soft and aromatic, about 8 minutes. Add most of the asparagus, reserving a small handful of asparagus tops for serving. Stir together and sprinkle in the salt and pepper. Cook until the spears have brightened, about 4 minutes.

2. Pour in the vegetable stock and bring the pot to a boil. Once the mixture is boiling, reduce the heat and simmer until the asparagus is tender, about 8 minutes.

3. Fold in the spinach and stir until it is wilted. Remove the soup from the heat and allow it to cool slightly.

4. Use an immersion blender to purée the soup, or transfer the soup to a blender to blend in batches. Pour the blended soup through a mesh sieve to catch excess pieces. Transfer the soup to a storage container and let it cool in the refrigerator for a couple of hours.

5. Transfer the cold soup to serving bowls. Garnish with the dill and asparagus tops.

TUXEDO TOMATO SOUP

· · · · · · ● ● ● ● ♥ ● ● ● ● · · ·

Presentation is so overrated. *Watch out as this Tuxedo Tomato Soup makes a splash, just like it did for Luc in his finest opera attire. This soup is simple but classic, and it will warm you even when you are left out in the cold by your boss.*

Makes 2 servings

· · · · · · · · · · · · · · · · ·

4 tablespoons unsalted butter

½ large onion, peeled and cut into wedges

1 (28-ounce) can whole peeled tomatoes

1½ cups low-sodium vegetable broth

½ teaspoon kosher salt

¼ teaspoon red pepper flakes, optional

4 basil leaves

½ teaspoon pecorino cheese

4 baguette slices, toasted

1. In a large saucepan, melt the butter over medium heat.

2. Add the onion, tomatoes, vegetable broth, and salt. Bring the pot to a simmer and then cook for 40 minutes, stirring occasionally.

3. Use an immersion blender to purée the soup, or transfer the soup to a blender to blend in batches.

4. Ladle the soup into 2 bowls. Garnish with the basil and pecorino. Serve with the toasted baguette slices.

MAD, MAD CARROTS

· · · · • • ⚫ ♥ ⚫ • • · · ·

The only thing more constant than Madeline Wheeler's go-getter attitude is her obsession with raw carrots. These Mad, Mad Carrots take their cues from Madeline's social media handle and give her addiction a much more satisfying spin.

Makes 6 servings
· · · · · · · · · · · · · · · ·

3 tablespoons extra-virgin olive oil

1 teaspoon fresh chopped thyme

½ teaspoon oregano

½ teaspoon kosher salt

2 pounds carrots, peeled and cut into 2-inch spears

1. Preheat the oven to 400°F. Prepare a baking sheet with parchment paper.

2. In a large mixing bowl, combine the olive oil, thyme, oregano, and salt. Toss in the carrots to coat.

3. Spread the carrots out evenly on the parchment-lined baking sheet.

4. Cover the carrots with foil and bake for 30 minutes.

FREE FOR LUNCH? NIÇOISE SALAD

Sylvie loves her outdoor lunches. Eventually, she transitions from begrudgingly allowing Emily to join to actually inviting her. Niçoise Salad is a classic French dish that's served cold, but it has heart.

Makes 4 servings

1 pound red potatoes

Kosher salt, to taste

6 ounces green beans

4 large eggs

8 cherry tomatoes, halved or quartered

1 cup herb dressing, divided

1 head Bibb lettuce, leaves separated

1 cup mixed olives, pitted

4 radishes, trimmed and sliced thin

2 small Persian cucumbers, sliced

2 (5-ounce) tins oil-packed tuna

1. In a large saucepan, cover the potatoes with water and season with the salt. Bring the potatoes to a simmer over medium-high heat and cook for 5 minutes or until you can easily pierce the potatoes with a fork. Drain the potatoes, slice into halves or quarters, and refrigerate to cool.

2. In a small saucepan, boil water. Add the green beans and blanch for 2 minutes. Drain the green beans and plunge them into cold water to cool. Set aside.

3. In a saucepan, cover the eggs with water and season with the salt. Bring the pot to a simmer, remove from the heat, and let the eggs sit in the warm water for 10 minutes. Remove and discard the shells, slice the eggs in half, then set aside.

4. In a small bowl, toss the tomatoes with ¼ cup of the herb dressing. Arrange the lettuce, potatoes, green beans, olives, radishes, cucumbers, and eggs on a serving plate. Top with the tuna and the marinated tomatoes. Drizzle the salad with the remaining dressing.

GIVE ME A SIGN CAESAR SALAD

· · · · · • ● ◉ ♥ ◉ ● • · · · ·

People-watching on a Parisian patio may just be one of life's greatest pleasures. Emily perused the menu for a twenty-Euro salad, but her takeaway was a know-it-all paramour. This Give Me a Sign Caesar Salad is a nod—or a gesture— toward the classic salad that never disappoints.

Makes 4 servings
· · · · · · · · · · · · · · · ·

2 small cloves garlic, minced

1 teaspoon anchovy paste

2 tablespoons fresh lemon juice

1 teaspoon Dijon mustard

1 teaspoon Worcestershire sauce

1 cup mayonnaise

¼ teaspoon salt

¼ teaspoon freshly ground black pepper

1 large head romaine lettuce, washed, dried, and torn into pieces

1 cup croutons

¼ cup shredded Parmesan

6–8 anchovy filets, optional

1. In a large bowl, whisk together the garlic, anchovy paste, lemon juice, Dijon mustard, and Worcestershire sauce. Add the mayonnaise, salt, and pepper, and continue whisking until blended.

2. Add the lettuce to the bowl and toss with tongs until evenly coated. Transfer the salad to a serving plate and top with the croutons, shredded Parmesan, and anchovy filets, if desired.

PARIS IS FOR CHEESE BOARDS

· · · ● ● ● ◉ ♥ ◉ ● ● ● · · ·

Emily knows that #ParisIsForCheeseLovers, but you can indulge in one of France's best exports anywhere. This gussied-up cheese board includes your favorite charcuterie, accompaniments, and sweet and savory touches for the perfect balance. If you can't find the recommended cheeses or meats, simply replace them with what's available and to your liking.

Makes 6 servings

· · · · · · · · · · · · · · · ·

1 (8-ounce) wedge Beaufort cheese

4 ounces Roquefort cheese

6–8 slices Emmental cheese

2 ounces Rosette de Lyon or other salami

4 ounces jambon de Bayonne or other cured ham

1 cup dried figs

1 cup trail mix

½ cup green olives, pitted

1 bunch red grapes, washed

1 bunch grape tomatoes, washed

1 small olive loaf, sliced

Assorted crackers and breadsticks

Honey, for drizzling

1 jar jam of choice

1. Assemble the ingredients on a large serving platter or board. Wrap a few breadsticks in the cured ham for easy snacking.

FRENCH ONION SOUP

················ ♥ ···········

The quintessential winter warmer, French Onion Soup speaks for itself. Emily might find this ultra-satisfying soup just a few cobblestones—or one flight of stairs—away.

Makes 4 servings
·················

2 tablespoons butter

4 large yellow onions, peeled and thinly sliced

½ teaspoon garlic powder

1 teaspoon black pepper

2 quarts beef broth

2 tablespoons Worcestershire sauce

1 cup dry white wine

1 tablespoon dry sherry

1 tablespoon all-purpose flour

¼ teaspoon kosher salt

8–10 slices toasted baguette

4 slices Gruyère cheese

1. In a large Dutch oven, melt the butter over medium heat. Stir in the onions, garlic powder, and black pepper. Cover and cook for 5 minutes, or until the onions have softened. Remove the lid and caramelize the onions, stirring occasionally, for 45 minutes.

2. In a separate pot, warm the beef broth and Worcestershire sauce.

3. When the onions have caramelized, pour in the wine and sherry, and bring the pot to a boil. Stir in the flour to thicken.

4. Stream in the warm broth and the salt. Boil, uncovered, for 10 minutes.

5. Preheat the broiler. Prepare a baking sheet with parchment paper.

6. Arrange 4 oven-safe bowls on the parchment-lined baking sheet.

7. Ladle the soup into the bowls. Top each with a slice of the toasted bread and a slice of cheese. Transfer the baking sheet to the oven and broil until the cheese has melted and is lightly browned.

ESCARGOTS DE BOURGOGNE

Get your tongs on classic Escargots de Bourgogne. This buttery and delicious starter is so good, you'll forget you are eating . . . snails. Don't forget to bring bread to soak up the parsley butter blend.

Makes 2 servings

12 escargots

2 cups kosher salt

1 clove garlic, peeled

1 stick (8 tablespoons) unsalted butter, softened

1½ teaspoons finely minced shallot

1 tablespoon finely chopped fresh flat-leaf parsley

¼ teaspoon kosher salt

¼ teaspoon black pepper

1 tablespoon dry white wine

1 baguette, for serving

1. Preheat the oven to 450°F.

2. Remove the escargots from their shells and rinse out the shells. Set the escargots aside. Create small mounds with the 2 cups of salt in a shallow baking dish. Arrange the shells on top of the mounds to keep them stable.

3. Mash the garlic to form a paste. In a medium bowl, combine the garlic paste, butter, shallot, parsley, ¼ teaspoon salt, and pepper. Pour in the wine and whisk until well combined.

4. Scoop half of the garlic mixture into the shells. Place the escargots back in their shells, and then top with the rest of the mixture.

5. Transfer the baking dish to the oven and bake for 4 to 6 minutes, or until the butter is bubbling. Serve with a toasted baguette.

TRÈS HOT DINNERS

LA PLOUC POULET

· · · · ● ● ● ♥ ● ● · · · ·

There's no burn quite so scorching as one branded by the staff of Savoir, and la plouc *is one of their best. This recipe is a spin on the classic French dish* coq au vin, *and even an American "hick" can make it. When you say* bonjour *to this cozy recipe, you'll be so pleased you won't even mind the nickname.*

Makes 4 servings
· · · · · · · · · · · · · · · ·

8 strips bacon, chopped

3½ pounds bone-in, skin-on chicken thighs and drumsticks

Kosher salt and freshly ground black pepper

4 cloves garlic, minced

2 shallots, peeled and quartered

1 bay leaf

6 sprigs thyme, divided

2 tablespoons tomato paste

3 large carrots, peeled and sliced

2 cups chicken stock

¼ cup brandy

½ (750-milliliter) bottle dry red wine

3 tablespoons salted butter, melted

3 tablespoons flour

1 pound cremini mushrooms, thickly sliced

½ pound frozen pearl onions

1. Preheat the oven to 350°F.

2. In a Dutch oven or large oven-safe skillet, cook the bacon over medium heat for 8 to 10 minutes, or until crisp. Transfer the bacon to a plate and reserve 2 tablespoons of bacon fat.

3. Season chicken with salt and pepper. Place the chicken in the pan and cook over medium heat or until browned, about 5 minutes. Work in batches, to avoid overcrowding the pan. Remove the chicken and set aside.

4. Add the garlic, shallots, bay leaf, 4 sprigs of thyme, tomato paste, and cooked bacon to the pan and stir for about 1 minute.

5. Return the chicken to the pan, skin up, and add the carrots, chicken stock, brandy, and wine. Once simmering, transfer the pan to the oven and braise for 30 minutes.

6. Remove the pan from the oven and place on the stovetop. In a small bowl, whisk the melted butter, flour, and ¼ cup of the liquid from the pan. Pour the mixture into the pan and combine.

7. Add the mushrooms and onions to the pan and cook, covered, for another 10 minutes or until the chicken is cooked through to 165°F. Remove the bay leaf and the cooked sprigs of thyme if desired. Garnish with the remaining fresh sprigs.

SURPRISINGLY TENDER STEAK AU POIVRE

· · · ● ● ● ♥ ● ● ● · · ·

The quickest way to a chef's heart is to insult his cooking, no? The Surprisingly Tender Steak au Poivre is a little lesson for Emily on what happens when you trust the one in the kitchen. Perfectly juicy and satisfying, this steak goes great with sautéed vegetables and mashed potatoes (page 81).

Makes 2 servings
· · · · · · · · · · · · · · · · ·

2 (6-ounce) medallion steaks, such as tenderloin or filet mignon

¼ teaspoon kosher salt

2 tablespoons whole peppercorns

1 tablespoon unsalted butter

1 teaspoon extra-virgin olive oil

⅓ cup Cognac, plus 1 teaspoon

1 cup heavy cream

1 pinch sea salt

2 sprigs rosemary

1. Let the steaks rest outside of the refrigerator for 30 minutes to 1 hour prior to cooking.

2. Sprinkle both sides of the steaks with salt. Crush the peppercorns and use them to coat the steaks on both sides. Set aside.

3. In a medium skillet over medium-high heat, melt the butter and olive oil. When the mixture begins to smoke, add the steaks to the pan and cook for 4 minutes on each side. Remove the pan from the heat and set the steaks aside. Discard the extra drippings but do not clean the pan.

4. In the same pan, add the Cognac and light it with a long match. Shake the pan and allow the flames to subside, and then return the pan to the heat. Pour in the cream and bring it to a boil. Whisk the mixture for 5 minutes. Add the final teaspoon of the Cognac and season with salt. Return the steaks to the pan and coat with the sauce. Plate the steaks with sides of your choice and garnish with the rosemary.

BOUILLABAISSE

· · · · ● ● ● ♥ ● ● ● · · ·

You can take the train on a weekend getaway to the beach with Mr. Wrong to get seafood, or you can make this sumptuous dish at home. These classic flavors warm the soul and will make you forget any embarrassing love triangles.

Makes 6 servings
· · · · · · · · · · · · · · · ·

4 tablespoons extra-virgin olive oil

1 yellow onion, peeled and diced

1 fennel bulb, trimmed and chopped

2 ribs celery, diced

1 carrot, peeled and diced

1 pound fingerling potatoes, sliced

4 cloves garlic, minced

2½ cups diced tomatoes

1 bay leaf

3 sprigs thyme

½ teaspoon saffron threads

4 cups fish broth

1½ pounds firm white fish, cut into 2-inch pieces

6 sea scallops

15 shrimp, deveined and shells removed

½ pound mussels, cleaned

1 baguette, for serving

1. In a large Dutch oven over medium heat, heat the olive oil. When the oil is shimmering, add the onion, fennel, celery, carrot, and potatoes.

2. Add garlic, tomatoes, bay leaf, thyme, and saffron. Cook for another 8 minutes, stirring occasionally. Pour in the fish broth and bring to a boil. When the potatoes are just about fork tender, add the fish and the scallops and reduce the heat. Simmer for 2 minutes, and then add the shrimp and mussels. Simmer for another 5 minutes until the shrimp is opaque and the mussel shells have opened. Remove and discard bay leaf.

3. Ladle into bowls and serve with bread.

CROQUE MADAM

· · · • • • ♥ • • • • · · ·

Only the French could elevate the grilled cheese to be so sophisticated. This sandwich is just as brunch-worthy as it is perfect for a night out after drinking too much Champère.

Makes 2 sandwiches

· · · · · · · · · · · · · · · ·

4 slices sourdough bread

3 tablespoons unsalted butter, softened, divided

1 tablespoon all-purpose flour

¾ cup whole milk

½ teaspoon kosher salt

¼ teaspoon black pepper

¼ cup shredded Gruyère cheese

4 slices ham

1 tablespoon Dijon mustard

2 slices Gouda cheese

2 large eggs

1 avocado, pitted and sliced

1. Preheat the broiler. Prepare a baking sheet with parchment paper.

2. Using 1 tablespoon of the butter, butter 1 side of each slice of bread. In a large skillet over medium-high heat, place the bread slices butter-side down and toast for 2 minutes or until golden brown.

3. In a small saucepan over medium heat, melt 1 tablespoon of butter. When the butter is bubbly, whisk in the flour until the mixture is golden, about 1 minute. Stir in the milk and bring the mixture to a simmer, whisking constantly. Reduce the heat to low and continue to whisk for about 3 minutes. Season with salt and pepper. Remove from the heat and stir in the Gruyère.

4. Assemble the sandwiches on the parchment-lined baking sheet: On two slices, toasted side down, spoon 2 tablespoons of the sauce to coat. Arrange the ham on both slices. Spread the mustard on the inside of the other 2 slices of toast. Close the sandwiches and top both with the slices of Gouda.

5. Spoon more of the sauce over the tops of the sandwiches. Transfer the baking sheet to the oven and broil for 5 minutes or until the cheese is lightly browned.

6. In a medium skillet over medium-high heat, heat 1 tablespoon of butter. Fry the eggs for about 3 minutes, flipping about halfway through.

7. Remove the baking sheet from the oven and plate the sandwiches. Top the sandwiches with the fried eggs. Garnish with the avocado slices.

LEEK TART FOR DINNER

· · · · · ● ● ♥ ● ● · · · · ·

How does anyone make leeks luxurious? Just ask Emily. While her mental wheels are turning about her latest promotional campaign, Gabriel muses about what she could possibly be whipping up with her bundle of leeks. This zucchini–leek tart is a savory, delicious way to celebrate the could-be next big thing.

Makes 1 tart
· · · · · · · · · · · · · · · ·

1 all-butter pie crust

1 tablespoon extra-virgin olive oil

1 medium leek, sliced

2 medium zucchinis, thinly sliced

¼ teaspoon kosher salt, divided

6 large eggs

¾ cup heavy cream

1 tablespoons chives

1½ cups shredded Gruyère cheese

¼ cup chopped fresh parsley

1. Prepare a 9-inch glass pie pan with 1 layer of pie crust and par-bake according to package instructions.

2. Preheat the oven to 350°F.

3. In a large skillet over medium-high heat, heat the olive oil. When the oil is shimmering, add the leek slices, 3 cups of the zucchini slices, and ⅛ teaspoon salt. Stir frequently for about 4 to 5 minutes, or until the vegetables soften. Remove the vegetables from the heat.

4. In a medium bowl, whisk together the eggs, heavy cream, chives, and ⅛ teaspoon salt. Set aside.

5. Spread half of the vegetables into the prepared pie pan and sprinkle with ¾ cup of the Gruyère. Spread the rest of the vegetable mixture over the top and sprinkle with ½ cup the Gruyère. Pour the egg mixture over the top to coat. Arrange the remaining zucchini slices in circles to decorate the top of the tart. Sprinkle with the remaining ¼ cup of Gruyère.

6. Transfer the tart to the oven and bake for 35 to 40 minutes, or until the tart has puffed in the center. Remove the tart from the oven and allow to cool briefly. Garnish with the parsley before cutting and serving.

DUCK CONFIT

Duck Confit is a French gold standard, and you may have noticed it listed while Gabriel reviews his menu. This dish isn't difficult, but it does require preparation a full day in advance—the anticipation makes the Voilà! *moment all the better. Serve with Mad, Mad Carrots (page 49) or a mixed green salad.*

Makes 2 servings

1½ teaspoons kosher salt

1 teaspoon freshly ground black pepper

1 bay leaf, torn

2 pounds duck legs

6 large shallots, peeled and quartered

1 small onion, peeled and cut into chunks

6 cloves garlic

½ bunch flat-leaf parsley with stems, torn

2 teaspoons whole black peppercorns

5 sprigs fresh thyme

1. In a small bowl, combine the salt, pepper, and bay leaf. Season the duck legs with the mixture. Place the duck legs in a baking dish in one layer, skin-side up.

2. In a food processor, blend the shallots, onion, garlic, and parsley until finely chopped. Coat the duck legs with the mixture, plus the peppercorns and the thyme. Seal the dish tightly with plastic wrap and refrigerate for 24 hours.

3. Preheat the oven to 325°F. Remove the duck legs from the dish, wash them with cold water to remove the excess seasoning, and pat dry.

4. Arrange the duck legs in an oven-safe skillet, fat-side down, in one layer. Heat the duck legs over medium-high heat until the fat begins to render. After 20 minutes, or when there is about ¼ inch of rendered duck fat, flip the legs and remove them from the heat. Cover the skillet with foil and transfer it to the oven.

5. Roast the duck for 2 hours. Remove the foil and roast 1 hour more or until the duck has turned golden brown. Remove the duck from the oven and plate according to your preference. Reserve the excess fat for future meals.

SEARED TURBOT

There's always a surprise buried in the conversations between our American in Paris and her French counterparts. When Emily gives Gabriel's menu a glance, Tronçon de Raie is one of many options. But let's skip the stingray and instead try this lemony Seared Turbot, shall we?

Makes 2 servings

4 turbot fillets

Kosher salt, to taste

Freshly ground black pepper, to taste

2 tablespoons vegetable oil

1 stick (8 tablespoons) unsalted butter, divided

½ cup dry white wine

¼ cup capers, drained

Juice of 1 lemon

1 pound steamed haricot verts, for serving

Zest of 1 lemon

4 sprigs thyme

1. Season the turbot with salt and pepper on both sides. In a large skillet over medium-high heat, heat the vegetable oil. When the oil is shimmering, add the turbot and half of the butter. Cook the turbot for 1 minute on each side or until golden brown. Transfer the turbot to a separate plate but keep the skillet on the heat.

2. Pour the wine into the pan to deglaze and reduce until the pan is nearly dry. Brown the rest of the butter in the pan, and then add the capers, lemon juice, and turbot fillets.

3. Spoon the sauce over the fish and warm it in the pan. Plate the turbot and haricot verts, and spoon more sauce over the top of the fish. Sprinkle with the lemon zest and garnish with the thyme.

BEEF BOURGUIGNON

· · · · • ● ♥ ● ● · · · ·

Pour yourself a glass of Burgundy while you enjoy this Burgundian beauty.
Let the warm aromas fill your senses as you consider the joys of cooking
a dish that is significantly less complicated than a love triangle.

Makes 6 servings
· · · · · · · · · · · · · · · ·

2 pounds boneless beef chuck
roast, trimmed and cut into
1-inch cubes

2 teaspoons kosher salt

1 teaspoon ground black
pepper

4 slices thick-cut bacon,
chopped

1 medium yellow onion,
peeled and roughly diced

2 cloves garlic, minced

1 (8-ounce) package button
mushrooms, cleaned and
halved

2 tablespoons tomato paste

2 cups beef broth

1 cup dry red wine

1 pound carrots, peeled and
sliced into medallions

2 tablespoons all-purpose flour

4 sprigs thyme

1 baguette, for serving

1. Season the beef with the salt and pepper.

2. In a large Dutch oven over medium-high heat, cook the bacon
for about 7 minutes or until the bacon begins to brown.

3. Add in the beef and cook for another 7 minutes or until
browned on all sides. Add the onion and cook for 2 minutes or
until lightly softened. Stir in the garlic and cook for 1 minute more.

4. Stir in the mushrooms and tomato paste. Cook for 4 minutes
and then pour in the broth, wine, and carrots. Bring the pot to a
boil. When the mixture is boiling, reduce the heat to low, cover,
and cook for 40 minutes or until the beef is tender.

5. Remove the lid and ladle ½ cup of broth into a bowl or
measuring cup. Add the flour, whisking until smooth, and pour the
mixture back into the pot. Stir continuously for 4 minutes or until
the sauce thickens a little.

6. Ladle the beef into bowls and garnish with the thyme. Serve
with the bread.

RATATOUILLE

· · · · • • • ❤ • • • • · · ·

Is it a delicious dish or is it fashion? Maybe it's both. There's nothing ringarde *about this gorgeous veggie treat, and it will satisfy your hunger while complementing your aesthetic.*

Makes 8 servings
· · · · · · · · · · · · · · · · ·

FOR THE RATATOUILLE

2 zucchinis

2 eggplants

2 yellow squashes

6 Roma tomatoes

2 tablespoons olive oil

1 medium white onion, peeled and diced

4 cloves garlic, minced

1 red bell pepper, seeded and diced

1 yellow bell pepper, seeded and diced

1 teaspoon kosher salt

1 teaspoon freshly ground black pepper

1 (28-ounce) can crushed tomatoes

2 sprigs thyme, torn

FOR THE SEASONING

4 tablespoons extra-virgin olive oil

1 clove garlic, minced

2 tablespoons chopped basil

2 teaspoons fresh thyme leaves

1. Preheat the oven to 375°F.

2. To make the ratatouille: Thinly slice the zucchini, eggplant, squash, and tomatoes using a mandoline or a sharp knife. Set aside.

3. In a medium skillet over medium-high heat, heat the oil. When the oil is shimmering, sauté the onion, garlic, and bell peppers for about 10 minutes. Sprinkle with the salt and pepper and then stir in the crushed tomatoes. Remove from the heat and transfer the mixture to a 12-inch pie pan or casserole dish. Smooth the mixture into the pan with a spatula.

4. Arrange the vegetables in a spiral on top of the sauce. Alternate the vegetable slices in a consistent pattern, starting from the edge of the pan and working toward the center.

5. To make the seasoning: In a small bowl, whisk together the olive oil, garlic, basil, and thyme. Drizzle the seasoning over the ratatouille.

6. Cover the pan with foil and transfer the ratatouille to the oven. Bake for 40 minutes, remove the foil, and continue to brown for another 20 minutes. Remove from the oven and garnish with the thyme sprigs before serving.

THANKS, MATE, BEEF TENDERLOIN

· · · ● ● ● ❤ ● ● ● · · ·

If you're going to introduce your Londoner beau to the French one who got away, make sure at least one of them is well fed. The Thanks, Mate, Beef Tenderloin is a nod to the meal Gabriel prepares when Emily introduces Alfie for the first time. The tenderloin is the star of the show and can be served with a variety of sides, like potatoes and sautéed veggies.

Makes 4 servings
· · · · · · · · · · · · · · · ·

2 pounds beef tenderloin, trimmed and tied

1 teaspoon kosher salt

1 teaspoon freshly ground black pepper

4 cups chicken stock

½ cup dry sherry

1 (7-ounce) can black truffle peelings

1. Preheat the oven to 500°F. Season the beef tenderloin with the salt and pepper and transfer to a roasting pan. Roast the tenderloin for 25 minutes for medium-rare.

2. While the tenderloin is roasting, prepare the truffle sauce. In a large pot over high heat, heat the chicken stock. When the stock has reduced to 1 cup, reduce the heat to medium and add the sherry and the entire truffle can. Allow the sauce to reduce until the mixture is slightly sticky. Remove from the heat.

3. Slice the tenderloin into medallions and arrange on a serving plate. Spoon the sauce over the tenderloin and serve.

TWINKLY LIGHTS ROAST CHICKEN

Birthdays are a great excuse to dazzle. Twinkly Lights Roast Chicken will do just that, but you don't have to wait for that one day a year. Celebrate in your finest fashion, like Emily in the park outside her door, and let this complete one-pan meal speak for itself.

Makes 8 servings

1 (5-pound) roasting chicken

1 lemon, quartered

1 head garlic, cut in half crosswise

6 sprigs rosemary, divided

2 tablespoons butter, softened

2 tablespoons honey

Kosher salt, to taste

Freshly ground black pepper, to taste

1 large yellow onion, peeled and thickly sliced

1 pound baby potatoes, halved

1 pound Brussels sprouts, trimmed and halved

Extra-virgin olive oil

1. Preheat the oven to 450°F.

2. Clean the chicken and remove the giblets. Stuff the inside of the chicken with the lemon, garlic, and 3 sprigs of the rosemary. Rub the outside of the chicken with the butter and honey, and season liberally with salt and pepper.

3. Place the chicken in a large roasting pan. Arrange the onion, potatoes, and Brussels sprouts in the roasting pan around the chicken. Drizzle with the olive oil and season with salt, pepper, and the rest of the rosemary, torn.

4. Roast the chicken for 10 to 15 minutes, and then reduce the heat to 350°F. Roast for 20 minutes per pound or until the internal temperature is 165°F, the skin is crispy, and the juices run clear.

5. Remove the chicken from the oven and let it rest for 10 to 20 minutes before serving.

CHICAGO DEEP DISH PIZZA

· · · · ● ● ● ♥ ● ● ● · · · ·

For Emily, nothing says home like Chicago Deep Dish Pizza. It's nothing fancy against the backdrop of the Eiffel Tower, but it's comforting and undeniably delicious.

Makes 2 pizzas
· · · · · · · · · · · · · · · · ·

FOR THE DOUGH

3¼ cups all-purpose flour

½ cup cornmeal

1¼ teaspoons salt

1 tablespoon granulated sugar

2¼ teaspoons instant or active dry yeast

1¼ cups lukewarm water

½ cup unsalted butter, divided (¼ cup melted, ¼ cup softened to room temperature)

2 tablespoons olive oil

FOR THE FILLING

4 cups pizza sauce

½ teaspoon crushed red pepper flakes, optional

2 tablespoons extra-virgin olive oil

1 small onion, peeled and diced

1 bell pepper, seeded and chopped

1. In the bowl of a stand mixer fitted with the dough hook attachment, mix together the flour, cornmeal, salt, sugar, and yeast. Add the lukewarm water and melted butter. Stir the ingredients on low speed until the dough begins to moisten. Continue to mix the dough or knead by hand until the dough is soft and pliable and pulls away from the sides of the mixing bowl. Remove the dough from the mixing bowl and form a ball.

2. Lightly grease a large mixing bowl with the olive oil. Place the dough inside the bowl and coat it with the olive oil. Cover the bowl and let the dough rise at a warm room temperature for 1 to 2 hours or until doubled in size.

3. On a lightly floured work surface, punch down the dough. Roll the dough into a 15 × 12-inch rectangle. Rub the softened butter on the surface of the dough, and then roll the dough up lengthwise like a log. Cut the dough in half, work the halves into balls, and place them back in the greased bowl. Cover the bowl and transfer to the refrigerator for 1 hour to rise.

4. To make the filling, first heat the pizza sauce in a medium saucepan on low heat. Add the red pepper flakes if desired. Simmer the sauce for 1 hour or until very thick and then remove it from the heat.

5. While the sauce is simmering, prepare the vegetables. In a skillet over medium heat, heat the olive oil. When the oil is shimmering, sauté the onion for 3 to 4 minutes. Add the pepper and mushrooms, sautéing for another 3 minutes or until the peppers have brightened but are still crisp. Remove from the heat and set aside.

1 (8-ounce) package cremini mushrooms, destemmed and chopped

2 cups shredded mozzarella

¼ cup pecorino cheese

Fresh basil, for garnish

Parsley, for garnish

6. Preheat the oven to 425°F. Prepare a baking sheet with parchment paper.

7. To assemble the pizzas, remove one of the balls of dough from the refrigerator. The dough should be puffy. On a lightly floured work surface, roll out the dough into a 12-inch circle and then place it in a 9 × 2-inch-deep cake pan. Use your fingers to conform the dough to the shape of the pan. Trim any excess dough off the edges of the pan. Repeat this process with the second ball of dough.

8. Lightly grease the top of the dough with olive oil. Scoop half of the vegetable mixture into the pizza pan and spread out evenly. Sprinkle with half of the mozzarella. Pour about half the sauce over the mixture, or any amount you desire. Sprinkle with half the pecorino. Repeat this process for the second pizza.

9. Place the pizzas on the baking sheet and transfer the baking sheet to the oven. Bake for 25 minutes or until the sauce is bubbling and the cheese is golden.

10. Remove the pizzas from the oven and let them cool for 5 to 10 minutes. Garnish with the basil and parsley before slicing and serving.

STEAK FRITES

*This dish is mouth-watering, but inspiringly easy. You'll be gliding around
your kitchen with the grace and stamina of Gabriel when he cooks for Emily.
Don't forget, there's no "Steak Frites" without Oui Fries (page 23).*

Makes 2 servings

2 rib eye steaks

5½ tablespoons unsalted
butter, divided (1½
tablespoons melted, 4
tablespoons softened to
room temperature)

Kosher salt, to taste

Freshly ground black pepper,
to taste

1 ounce Roquefort cheese,
room temperature

1 tablespoon extra-virgin
olive oil

1 pinch teaspoon sea salt

1. Rub the steaks with the melted butter and season with salt
and pepper.

2. In a small bowl, blend the softened butter with the Roquefort
until smooth.

3. In a medium skillet over medium-high heat, heat the olive oil.
When the oil is shimmering, add the steaks to the pan and cook
for 4 minutes on each side.

4. Plate the steaks. Sprinkle the sea salt on the steaks, and then
spoon the Roquefort mixture on top for serving.

CROQUE MONSIEUR

· · · · ● ● ❤ ● ● · · · ·

Not to be confused with or outshone by the Croque Madam, this sophisticated sandwich is a wonder unto itself. Bathed in a luxurious béchamel, it's steps above American grilled cheese, and it knows it.

Makes 2 sandwiches
· · · · · · · · · · · · · · ·

FOR THE BÉCHAMEL

4 tablespoons unsalted butter

¼ cup all-purpose flour

1½ cups whole milk

Kosher salt, to taste

Freshly ground black pepper, to taste

¼ teaspoon Dijon mustard

1 pinch ground nutmeg

FOR THE SANDWICHES

4 slices sourdough bread

4 slices ham

1¼ cups shredded Gruyère cheese

¼ cup freshly grated Parmesan cheese

1. Preheat the oven to 425°F. Prepare a baking sheet with parchment paper.

2. In a small saucepan over medium heat, melt the butter. When the butter is bubbly, whisk in the flour until the mixture is golden, about 1 minute. Stir in the milk and bring the mixture to a simmer, whisking constantly. Reduce the heat to low and continue to whisk for about 3 minutes. Season with salt and pepper. Remove from heat and whisk in the mustard and nutmeg. Set aside.

3. Arrange the bread on the parchment-lined baking sheet. Spread a layer of the béchamel sauce on each slice of sourdough. Arrange the ham on two slices and sprinkle with some of the Gruyère and Parmesan. Close the sandwiches, béchamel-side up. Sprinkle them with the rest of the Gruyère and Parmesan.

4. Transfer the baking sheet to the oven and bake for 5 minutes. Switch the oven to broil, and broil until the cheese is golden brown.

5. Remove the baking sheet from the oven and plate the sandwiches.

AFFAIR OF LEGENDS LAMB SHANKS

· · · · • • ◉ ◉ ◉ ♥ ◉ ◉ ◉ • • · · ·

Emily is a fixer by nature. When Emily confuses the dates of a business dinner, Sylvie is ready to watch her crash and burn. But it's Emily's charm and quick thinking that get her out of this would-be disaster. Gabriel prepares a show-stopping dinner for the "affair of legends," including sumptuous lamb shanks and mashed potatoes.

Makes 6 servings

· · · · · · · · · · · · · · · · ·

FOR THE LAMB SHANKS

6 lamb shanks

Kosher salt, to taste

Freshly ground black pepper, to taste

2 tablespoons extra-virgin olive oil

3 large carrots, sliced into medallions

2 ribs celery, diced

2 yellow onions, peeled and chopped

10 cloves garlic, minced

1 (750-milliliter) bottle dry red wine

1 (28-ounce) can whole peeled tomatoes

1 (10.5-ounce) can beef broth

1 (10.5-ounce) can condensed chicken broth

3 sprigs fresh thyme, stems removed and chopped

3 sprigs fresh rosemary, stems removed and chopped

1. To make the lamb shanks, first season them with salt and pepper. In a Dutch oven or large pot over medium-high heat, heat the oil. Working in batches, cook the lamb shanks, browning them on all sides, for about 8 minutes. Remove the meat from the pan and set aside.

2. Over medium heat, sauté the carrots, celery, onions, and garlic in the same pan you used for the lamb shanks. Cook for about 10 minutes or until the mixture is golden brown. Stir in the wine, tomatoes, beef broth, chicken broth, thyme, and rosemary.

3. Transfer the lamb shanks back to the pan and coat with the liquid. Bring the contents to a boil, cover, and then reduce the heat to medium-low. Simmer for 2 hours, or until the meat is pull-apart tender.

4. After the lamb shanks have been cooking for 1 hour, prepare the mashed potatoes. Place the potatoes in a large pot and cover with cold water. Add the salt and bring the pot to a simmer. Cook until the potatoes are fork tender, about 45 minutes.

5. Drain the potatoes and return them to the pot. On low heat, add the butter, sour cream, and whole milk. Mash with a potato masher or fork, turning the heat off once the butter is nearly melted. Season with salt and pepper and transfer to a serving bowl.

FOR THE MASHED POTATOES

2 pounds Yukon gold
　potatoes, peeled

2 tablespoons kosher salt,
　plus more to taste

1 stick (8 tablespoons)
　unsalted butter

½ cup sour cream

½ cup whole milk

Freshly ground black pepper,
　to taste

6. Remove the lid from the lamb shanks and simmer for another 20 minutes. Remove the lamb shanks and transfer them to a serving plate. Boil the sauce to thicken for another 15 minutes, and then pour the sauce into a bowl with a serving spoon.

7. At serving, guests can spoon the sauce over their mashed potatoes and lamb shanks.

Chapter Four

UN PETIT

Plaisir Sweets

· · · · ● ● ● ♥ ● ● ● · · · · ·

PARISIAN DREAM MADELEINES

Emily's life in Paris is a dream, but it started off as Madeline's.
These Parisian Dream Madeleines are a tribute to the boss whose changed
plans led the way for Emily to dream bigger and sweeter.

Makes 12 madeleines

¼ cup unsalted butter, melted,
plus more for greasing

2 large eggs

¾ teaspoon vanilla extract

⅛ teaspoon salt

⅓ cup granulated sugar

½ cup all-purpose flour

1 tablespoon lemon zest

Honey, for serving

1. Preheat the oven to 375°F. Grease a (12-cake, 3-inch) madeleine mold with butter and dust with flour.

2. In a small mixing bowl, beat the eggs, vanilla, and salt. Gradually add the sugar and beat continuously for 5 to 10 minutes or until the mixture has thickened.

3. Gradually sift the flour into the egg mixture to combine. Fold in the lemon zest and the melted butter.

4. Spoon the batter into the madeleine molds, allowing the batter to mound. Bake for 15 minutes or until the madeleines are golden and springy. Transfer to a serving plate and serve with honey.

BERRY HUNGRY STRAWBERRY ICE CREAM

· · · ● ● ● ♥ ● ● ● · ·

Head off to that influencer brunch, snap some glam shots against a
strawberry wall, and then dive into the Berry Hungry Strawberry Ice Cream.
This creamy treat is just the thing to boost your (sugar) status.

Makes 10 cups
· · · · · · · · · · · · · · · ·

4 tablespoons lemon juice

2 tablespoons honey

3 cups fresh strawberries, hulled and diced, plus more for serving

½ cups granulated sugar

1½ cups whole milk

2¾ cups heavy cream

2 teaspoons vanilla extract

2–4 drops red food coloring, optional

1. In a large bowl, whisk the lemon juice and honey. Mix in the strawberries and granulated sugar. Let sit for 20 minutes. Strain the berries and reserve the juices. Divide the berries in half, setting one half aside.

2. Mash the other half of the berries in a large mixing bowl. Combine the mashed strawberries with the whole milk, heavy cream, vanilla extract, and food coloring (if using).

3. Pour the mixture into an ice cream maker and follow the manufacturer's instructions.

4. When the ice cream is finished, transfer to a container and stir in the reserved strawberries. Freeze for another 2 hours before serving. Garnish with reserved strawberries.

POACHED APRICOTS

· · · • • ⦿ ♥ ⦿ • • • · · ·

Sweet like candy or a wealth of springtime romances, a bowl of Poached Apricots is an unassuming stunner. This traditional dessert is big on flavor but has no need for try-hard flair. Save that for the layer cakes.

Makes 6 apricots

· · · · · · · · · · · · · · · ·

3 cups water

¼ cup plus 1 tablespoon honey

4 (3-inch) strips orange peel

6 medium-ripe apricots, pitted and quartered

1. In a medium saucepan over high heat, bring the water, honey, and orange peel to an active simmer. Add the apricots and be sure to submerge them in the liquid. Reduce the heat to a light simmer and cook until the apricots are tender, about 3 minutes.

2. With a slotted spoon, transfer the apricots to serving dishes. Coat them with just enough liquid to cover them. For the remaining liquid in the saucepan, increase the heat to medium-high. Let the liquid reduce by half for about 10 minutes, or until the liquid is syrupy.

3. Strain the syrup into the serving dishes. Refrigerate for 1 hour and then serve.

BETRAYAL BELGIAN CHOCOLATE CAKE

· · · ● ● ● ♥ ● ● ● · · ·

Preparing a gorgeous, multilayered chocolate cake for your . . . friend? This cake is a dead giveaway of a secret love, even if a certain chef hasn't admitted it to himself. The layers of chocolate are rich and unforgettable, just like Emily's birthday party.

Makes 12 servings

· · · · · · · · · · · · · · · ·

FOR THE CAKE

1¾ cups all-purpose flour

¾ cup unsweetened cocoa powder

1¾ cups granulated sugar

2 teaspoons baking soda

1 teaspoon baking powder

1 teaspoon salt

2 teaspoons espresso powder

½ cup vegetable oil

2 large eggs

¾ cup sour cream

½ cup buttermilk

2 teaspoons vanilla extract

½ cup hot water

1. Preheat the oven to 350°F. Grease four 9-inch cake pans. Line the cake pans with parchment paper rounds and then grease the surface of the paper.

2. Begin the cake. In a large bowl, combine the flour, cocoa powder, sugar, baking soda, baking powder, salt, and espresso powder. Set the bowl aside.

3. In the bowl of a stand mixer fitted with the whisk attachment, mix the oil, eggs, and sour cream on medium-high speed until combined. Stream in the buttermilk and the vanilla extract. Add the flour mixture and then the hot water. Beat on a low speed until well combined.

4. Divide the batter evenly among the baking pans. Transfer the pans to the oven and bake for 20 minutes or until a toothpick inserted in the center of the cake comes out clean. Remove the pans from the oven and allow the cakes to cool.

5. To prepare the chocolate mousse, start by whisking together the hot water and cocoa powder.

6. In a medium bowl, microwave the chocolate pieces in 20-second intervals. Stir between each interval and melt until there are only a few chunks left. Stir until the last chunks melt.

7. Stream the hot water mixture into the melted chocolate and stir. Set the bowl aside.

FOR THE CHOCOLATE MOUSSE

½ cup hot water

¼ cup unsweetened cocoa powder

2 (4-ounce) semisweet chocolate bars, chopped

2 cups heavy cream

2 tablespoons powdered sugar

½ teaspoon pure vanilla extract

FOR THE CHOCOLATE GANACHE

1 cup heavy cream

2 (4-ounce) semisweet chocolate bars, chopped

8. Using a stand mixer fitted with a whisk attachment, whip the heavy cream, powdered sugar, and vanilla extract on medium-high speed until soft peaks form.

9. Gently add the chocolate mixture to the cream mixture and gently fold together. Do not overmix. Cover the mousse and transfer to the refrigerator to chill for at least 2 hours.

10. When the mousse has chilled, assemble the layers. If the cakes need leveling, use a serrated bread knife to slice a thin layer off the tops of the cakes to make the surfaces smooth and flat. Place the first layer on a cake stand or serving plate. Using a rubber spatula, spread the chocolate mousse on the cake in a thick layer. Repeat this process with the remaining layers, reserving a large spoonful of the mousse to spread thinly on the top surface and outsides of the cake as a primer for the ganache. Transfer the cake to the refrigerator and chill for at least 1 hour.

11. To prepare the chocolate ganache, heat the cream in a small saucepan over medium heat. Bring the cream to a simmer. Pour the hot cream into a medium bowl with the chocolate pieces. Let the chocolate soften for 2 minutes. Gently stir the mixture until smooth, then let the ganache cool for 20 minutes.

12. Spread the chocolate ganache evenly over the surface of the cake. Decorate the cake as desired.

STRAWBERRY ANGEL CAKE

· · · · ● ● ● ♥ ● ● ● · · · ·

Strawberries are in season with the heavenly Strawberry Angel Cake.
Boost your mood and your socials with this light and airy dessert.

Makes 1 cake
· · · · · · · · · · · · · · · ·

FOR THE CAKE

1½ cups granulated sugar, divided

1 cup cake flour

12 egg whites, room temperature

1 teaspoon cream of tartar

½ teaspoon coarse kosher salt

1 tablespoon orange zest

2 teaspoons vanilla extract

FOR THE SAUCE

1 cup fresh strawberries, plus more for serving

2 tablespoons raw honey

Whipped cream, for serving

1. Preheat the oven to 325°F. Sift ¾ cup of the sugar and the cake flour together.

2. Using an electric hand mixer on low speed in a large bowl, beat the egg whites until they begin to foam. Add the cream of tartar and salt, and increase the speed of the mixer to medium-high. Gradually add the rest of the sugar and beat until stiff peaks form. Using a rubber spatula, fold in the orange zest and the vanilla extract.

3. Gently add the flour mixture to the meringue and fold together until mixed. Do not overmix.

4. Transfer the batter to an angel food cake pan. Bake the cake for 45 to 55 minutes, or until a toothpick comes out clean.

5. Invert the angel food cake pan over a mug or wine bottle. Let the cake cool for 2 hours inside the pan. This will allow air to circulate and prevent the cake from becoming too soggy.

6. Next, make the strawberry sauce. In a small saucepan over medium-high heat, bring the strawberries and honey to a boil. Reduce the heat and allow the sauce to simmer for 5 minutes. Transfer the sauce to a bowl and allow it to cool.

7. When serving, drizzle each piece of cake with the sauce and add several dollops of the whipped cream. Garnish with fresh strawberries.

RASPBERRY MILLE-FEUILLE

· · · · ● ● ◉ ❤ ◉ ● ● · · · ·

A cuter pastry, there never was. Raspberry Mille-Feuille is French elegance and precious attention to detail all wrapped into one beautiful little package. This surprisingly easy-to-make stack of cream, fresh raspberries, and crisp pastry offers the perfect balance of texture and sweetness.

Makes 9 servings

· · · · · · · · · · · · · · · · ·

FOR THE PASTRY CREAM

2 cups whole milk

1 teaspoon vanilla extract

⅔ cup granulated sugar

¼ cup cornstarch

6 large egg yolks

1 tablespoon unsalted butter, cold

½ cup heavy whipping cream

3 tablespoons powdered sugar

FOR THE PASTRY LAYERS

2 sheets puff pastry

FOR ASSEMBLING

3 cups fresh raspberries

Mint leaves, for garnish

1. To make the pastry cream, bring the milk and the vanilla to a boil in a medium saucepan over medium-high heat. Once it has boiled, let it rest for 15 minutes.

2. In a medium bowl, combine the sugar and cornstarch. Whisk in the egg yolks and beat until the mixture is fluffy. Stream in ¼ cup of the milk mixture to the bowl. Once combined, continue to stream in the rest of the milk. Return the mixture to the pot and place over medium-high heat. Continue whisking as the mixture comes to a boil and thickens, about 3 to 5 minutes. Transfer the pastry cream to a bowl through a fine mesh sieve, and beat in the butter until smooth. Cover tightly with plastic wrap, and refrigerate for at least 3 hours Transfer the pastry cream to a bowl, cover tightly with plastic wrap, and refrigerate.

3. Preheat the oven to 400°F. Prepare a baking sheet with parchment paper. Roll the puff pastry out to be about ¹⁄₁₆-inch thin and use a pizza cutter to slice the pastry into 2 × 4-inch pieces.

4. Transfer the puff pastry to the parchment-lined baking sheet, leaving ½ inch between each piece. Place a second sheet of parchment paper over this layer and place a second baking sheet on top to prevent the pastry from rising too much. Bake the pastry for 10 to 15 minutes, or until golden brown. Rotate the baking sheets halfway through. Cool the pastries and repeat with the second piece of puff pastry dough.

5. To make the whipped cream, combine the heavy cream and the powdered sugar in a small bowl. Using an electric hand mixer, whisk the cream and sugar on high speed until stiff peaks begin to form.

6. To assemble the mille-feuille, remove the fully chilled pastry cream from the refrigerator and whip it once more. Combine ½ cup of the whipped cream with the pastry cream. Fold in the rest of the whipped cream, and then transfer it to a piping bag with a round tip.

7. To decorate the pastry, neatly pipe the pastry cream and add raspberries in an every-other sequence. Add the second pastry layer, reversing the order. When add the last pastry layer layer, neatly pipe only dollops of the pastry cream onto the pastry. Top this layer with more raspberries and garnish with a sprig of mint.

TARTE TROPÉZIENNE

· · · · • • ● 🖤 ● • • • · · ·

A weekend in Saint-Tropez sounds divine, but Mindy and Emily find that it's a little
more complicated. Walking along café-lined streets, Mindy reminisces sharing
Tarte Tropézienne with her father years earlier. This satisfying brioche is perfect
as a sweet snack, a complete dessert, or as wistful nostalgia.

Makes 1 cake

· · · · · · · · · · · · · · · ·

FOR THE CAKE

2½ teaspoons active dry yeast

⅓ cup warm whole milk

2 cups all-purpose flour

3 tablespoons sugar

2 large eggs, lightly beaten

½ teaspoon sea salt

2 teaspoons dark rum

1 teaspoon vanilla extract

7 tablespoons unsalted butter,
   softened

1 large egg

1 teaspoon water

1 dash pearl sugar

1. To make the cake, combine the yeast and the warm milk in a small bowl. Allow the yeast to bubble.

2. In the bowl of a stand mixer fitted with the paddle attachment, combine the flour and the sugar on low speed. Add the yeast mixture and beat to incorporate it until the dough is shaggy. Gradually add the eggs one at a time, followed by the salt, rum, and vanilla extract. Increase the speed and scrape down the sides of the bowl as needed. Mix for 5 to 8 minutes or until the dough is smooth and separates from the sides of the bowl. Add the butter in chunks and mix for 8 to 10 minutes or until the dough is smooth and wraps around the paddle.

3. Transfer the dough to a large bowl. Using your hands, scoop up the dough and then let it drop back into the bowl. Repeat this process so that the dough rounds and slightly pancakes.

4. Cover the bowl with plastic wrap and let the dough rise at a warm room temperature for 2 to 3 hours or until it has doubled in size.

5. When the dough has risen, scoop up the dough and then let it drop back into the bowl. Repeat this process so that the dough rounds and slightly pancakes. Cover the bowl with plastic wrap and transfer it to the freezer for 30 minutes, then transfer the bowl to the refrigerator for 2 more hours.

6. When the dough is ready, prepare a baking sheet with parchment paper.

FOR THE PASTRY CREAM

1½ cups whole milk

4 large egg yolks

⅓ cup granulated sugar

¼ cup cornstarch

1 teaspoon sea salt

1 tablespoon vanilla extract

6 tablespoons unsalted butter, sliced into pats

¼ cup very cold heavy cream

7. On a lightly floured work surface, pat the dough and sprinkle flour on the top. Roll the dough out to a 10-inch circle. Transfer the dough to the baking sheet and cover with plastic wrap and let the dough rest in a warm room temperature for 1 hour.

8. While the dough is resting, make the pastry cream filling. In a medium saucepan, bring the milk to a boil. In a medium bowl, whisk together the yolks, sugar, cornstarch, and salt. Stream in half of the hot milk while whisking constantly. When the mixture is warm, stream in the rest of the milk and the vanilla extract. Transfer the mixture back to the saucepan and return to a boil while whisking continuously. Continue whisking for an additional 1 to 2 minutes after it begins to boil.

9. Scrape the pastry cream into a bowl and let it cool for 10 minutes. Blend in the butter a few pats at a time until well combined. Wrap with plastic wrap, allowing the wrap to smooth out the surface of the cream. Transfer the pastry cream to the refrigerator to chill for at least 2 hours.

10. Preheat the oven to 400°F. Place an oven rack in the center of the oven.

11. In a small bowl, whisk the egg and the water to make an egg wash. Brush the top of the dough with the egg wash. Sprinkle the pearl sugar on top of the dough.

12. Transfer the baking sheet to the oven and reduce the temperature to 350°F. Bake the cake for 10 minutes and then rotate the baking sheet. Bake for another 10 to 15 minutes. Remove the cake from the oven and allow it to cool on a cooling rack.

13. In a large bowl, whip the very cold heavy cream until it forms peaks. Give the pastry cream a whisk and then fold in the whipped cream with a rubber spatula.

14. When the cake has cooled, slowly and smoothly slice the cake horizontally using a serrated bread knife. Transfer the bottom layer to a serving plate. Spread the pastry cream on the cake and then replace the top. Let the cake cool in the refrigerator to set for at least 1 hour before serving.

SKOKIE, IL, USA FUNFETTI CUPCAKES

Care packages from Skokie, IL, USA bring perks—even in France—and one such perk is a box of Funfetti cupcakes. A dessert as peppy and earnest as Emily, this rainbow of fun will always feel like home.

Makes 20 cupcakes

FOR THE CUPCAKES

1½ cups all-purpose flour

¾ cup granulated sugar

1¼ teaspoons baking powder

½ teaspoon kosher salt

½ cup unsalted butter, sliced into pats

2 large eggs

½ cup whole milk

1½ teaspoons vanilla extract

⅓ cup rainbow sprinkles

FOR THE BUTTERCREAM

1 cup unsalted butter

3 cups powdered sugar

1 cup marshmallow creme

1 tablespoon vanilla extract

Star sprinkles, for decorating

1. Preheat the oven to 350°F. Prepare 2 cupcake pans with 20 colorful cupcake liners.

2. In the bowl of a stand mixer fitted with the paddle attachment, combine the flour, sugar, baking powder, and salt. Add the butter and mix on low until the mixture is crumbly.

3. Add the eggs one at a time and scrape down the sides of the bowl as needed. Stream in the milk and vanilla until well combined. Fold in the rainbow sprinkles with a rubber spatula.

4. Fill the cupcake liners about two-thirds full. Bake the cupcakes for 15 to 20 minutes, or until a toothpick comes out clean. Let the cupcakes cool before frosting.

5. Next, make the buttercream frosting. In the bowl of a stand mixer fitted with the mixer attachment, cream the butter until it is fluffy. Scrape down the sides of the bowl as needed. Gradually incorporate the powdered sugar, marshmallow creme, and vanilla. Mix for about 2 minutes or until fluffy.

6. Transfer the frosting to a piping bag with a star tip. Neatly pipe spirals onto the cupcakes, working from the outside in. Sprinkle the cupcakes with the star sprinkles.

PETIT PLAISIR MACARONS

· · · • ● ◉ ♥ ◉ ● • · · ·

As Gabriel knows, certain fast-food empires are nothing to stick up your nose at.
In fact, some pastry sections under these golden arches are very refined. For
Petit Plaisir Macarons, you can split up the batter to make multiple pastel
colors, or just choose the color you like best for the whole batch.

Makes 40 macarons

· · · · · · · · · · · · · · · · ·

FOR THE MACARONS

1 cup almond flour

1⅔ cups powdered sugar

2 teaspoons vanilla powder

3 egg whites, room
   temperature

¼ cup granulated sugar

Pastel food coloring, optional

FOR THE BUTTERCREAM

1 cup unsalted butter

3 cups powdered sugar

1 teaspoon vanilla extract

1–3 tablespoons cream

1. Prepare a baking sheet with parchment paper.

2. In a small bowl, combine the almond flour, powdered sugar, and vanilla powder.

3. Using an electric hand mixer on medium-high speed, beat the egg whites. When the egg whites are foamy, gradually add in the granulated sugar and beat until stiff peaks form. Fold in the food coloring, if using.

4. Preheat the oven to 285°F.

5. Gently add the flour mixture to the meringue and fold together until mixed. Do not overmix.

6. Transfer the batter to a piping bag with a round tip. Neatly pipe 2-inch dollops of the batter onto the parchment-paper-lined baking sheet.

7. Using a wet finger, smooth any batter tips from the piping bag so that the dollops are rounded.

8. Bake the macarons for 10 minutes or until the batter loses its sheen and the edges begin to shrink. When the macarons are finished, remove them from the oven and allow them to cool.

9. To make the buttercream frosting, combine the butter, powdered sugar, vanilla extract, and 1 tablespoon of cream in a large bowl.

10. Transfer the buttercream to a piping bag with a round tip. Neatly pipe dollops of the buttercream onto the undersides of half of the macarons. Top each frosted layer with another macaron.

VERY SATISFYING CRÈME BRÛLÉE

· · · · · ● ● ♥ ● ● · · · · ·

If you are teetering toward a breakdown, take a little advice from Pierre. When this fashion designer thinks he's on the edge of ruin, a little smash of a spoon and the crack of sugar soothes his anxiety. This Very Satisfying Crème Brûlée is just the treat.

Makes 4 custards
· · · · · · · · · · · · · · · ·

2 cups heavy cream

⅛ teaspoon salt

1 teaspoon vanilla extract

5 egg yolks

½ cup sugar, plus extra for topping

1. Preheat the oven to 325°F. In a saucepan over low heat, warm the cream and salt. Add the vanilla extract, stir, and then remove the mixture from the heat for 15 minutes.

2. In a medium bowl, whisk together the egg yolks and sugar until blended and the mixture begins to lighten in color. Stream in the cream mixture and stir continuously. Place four oven-safe ramekins in a baking dish, and then divide the cream mixture among the ramekins.

3. Fill the baking dish with boiling water up to the halfway point of the sides of the ramekins. Transfer to the oven and bake for 30 to 40 minutes or until the custard is not quite set. Remove from the oven, allow to cool, and then refrigerate for several hours.

4. For serving, sprinkle a teaspoon of sugar on top of each of the custards. Place the ramekins a few inches under the broiler for about 5 minutes, or until the sugar is melted and has hardened into a shell.

QUELLE SURPRISE COOKIES

Hoping to land a deal? Offer incentive. Hoping to land a deal with your hot neighbor with whom you have a will-they, won't-they romance? Offer the Quelle Surprise Cookies. Emily is nothing short of surprised when she sees Gabriel at Savoir, and these cookies are sitting on the table to ease the tension.

Makes 24–36 cookies

3 large eggs

¾ cup granulated sugar

1 cup melted unsalted butter, cooled to room temperature

2 teaspoons vanilla extract

4 cups all-purpose flour

1 teaspoon baking powder

1 (12-ounce) jar apricot jam

Powdered sugar, for sprinkling

1. Preheat the oven to 350°F. Prepare a baking sheet with parchment paper.

2. Using an electric hand mixer on medium-high speed, beat the eggs and sugar. When the eggs are foamy, whisk in the melted butter and then the vanilla until combined.

3. In a medium bowl, combine the flour and the baking powder. Stream in the egg mixture to form a firm dough.

4. Divide the dough into three sections. On the parchment-lined baking sheet with a sprinkling of flour, roll out one section of the dough to be ⅛-inch thick. Using a 2-inch ribboned cookie cutter, cut as many cookies as space will allow. Using a smaller cookie cutter or a sharp knife, cut smaller holes into the center of half of the cookies. Remove the center pieces of dough as well as that excess dough around the cookies.

5. Bake the cookies in the oven for 7 to 9 minutes or until lightly golden. Repeat this process with the remaining dough. Utilize the excess dough by rerolling, cutting more cookies, and baking as instructed.

6. Spoon dollops of the jam onto the whole cookies. Top the whole cookies with the cookies with holes. Sprinkle the cookies with powdered sugar before serving.

CHUNKY "UNSALTED" PEANUT BUTTER COOKIES

· · · · · ● ◉ ♥ ◉ ● · · · · ·

There are few things Emily misses from the good ol' U.S. of A., but one of them is chunky unsalted peanut butter. In this recipe, you will need to use salted peanut butter for the cookie flavor to really explode, but at least it won't be exploding all over your belongings.

Makes 24 cookies

· · · · · · · · · · · · · · · ·

1⅓ cups all-purpose flour

½ teaspoon baking soda

1 stick (8 tablespoons) unsalted butter, softened

½ cup granulated sugar

½ cup packed light brown sugar

¾ teaspoon kosher salt

1 large egg

1 teaspoon vanilla extract

⅔ cup salted chunky peanut butter

1 cup semisweet chocolate chips

½ cup unsalted peanuts

1. In a medium bowl, combine the flour and baking soda. In the bowl of a stand mixer fitted with the paddle attachment, combine the butter, granulated sugar, brown sugar, and salt. Beat on medium for about 4 minutes, scraping down the sides with the paddle as necessary. Add the egg and the vanilla extract and beat until combined, then add the peanut butter. When the mixture is smooth and fluffy, add the flour mixture and mix until combined.

2. Release the bowl from the stand mixer and fold in the chocolate chips and the peanuts using a rubber spatula. Prepare a baking sheet with parchment paper. Spoon the dough onto the baking sheet in mounds. Transfer the baking sheet to the refrigerator for 40 minutes to chill the dough.

3. Preheat the oven to 350°F and evenly space the oven racks. Prepare another baking sheet with parchment paper. Remove the dough from the refrigerator and divide the mounds between the 2 baking sheets, spacing the cookies evenly apart. Use a fork to flatten each mound of dough and to create hatch mark imprints.

4. Transfer the baking sheets to the oven and bake for 10 minutes. Rotate the baking sheets and then bake for 4 minutes more or until the cookies are lightly golden. Remove the baking sheets from the oven and allow the cookies to cool on wire racks.

PALMIERS

These petite palmiers are all too cute. Surprisingly easy for a French pastry,
they can be whipped up in no time, and you'll feel like you've hit your local pâtisserie.

Makes 40 palmiers

2 cups granulated sugar

⅛ teaspoon kosher salt

2 sheets puff pastry

1. Preheat the oven to 450°F. Prepare a baking sheet with parchment paper.

2. In a small bowl, combine the sugar and the salt.

3. On a clean board or surface, spread out 1 cup of the sugar mixture.

4. Unroll the puff pastry sheets onto the same surface and spread out ½ cup of the sugar mixture evenly across the pastry. Roll out one of the sheets to be 13 × 13 inches so that the sugar firmly clings to the pastry.

5. Fold the left and right sides of the dough a quarter of the way toward the center. Fold these sections to meet at the center, then fold the sections so that they close like a book, but don't pinch them too hard.

6. Slice the dough crosswise into ⅜-inch slices and place the slices, cut-side up, on the parchment-paper-lined baking sheets.

7. Repeat this process for the second pastry sheet.

8. Bake the palmiers for 6 minutes, until they begin to brown on the bottom. Flip the palmiers and bake for another 3 to 5 minutes. Remove them from the oven and allow them to cool.

CHOCOLATE MOUSSE

· · · · ● ● ● ♥ ● ● ● · · ·

Embrace extravagance. With this decadent Chocolate Mousse, step into Sylvie's stilettos and vie for only the most luxurious indulgences. This sweet treat is simple, but so satisfying.

Makes 6 servings
· · · · · · · · · · · · · · ·

3 tablespoons unsalted butter

6 ounces semisweet chocolate, broken into pieces

3 large eggs, separated

½ teaspoon cream of tartar

¼ cup plus 2 tablespoons sugar

½ teaspoon vanilla extract

½ cup heavy whipping cream

Chocolate shavings

1. In a medium bowl, microwave the butter and chocolate pieces in 20-second intervals. Stir between each interval and melt until there are only a few chunks left. Stir until the last chunks melt.

2. Allow the chocolate to cool for a few minutes and then whisk in the egg yolks one at a time. Set the mixture aside.

3. Using an electric hand mixer on medium-high speed, beat the egg whites. When the egg whites are foamy, add the cream of tartar. Gradually add ¼ cup of the sugar and beat until stiff peaks form. Gently fold the egg whites into the chocolate mixture.

4. Divide the mousse among 6 glass dishes. Cover the dishes and transfer them to the refrigerator to chill for at least 2 hours.

5. In a small bowl, combine the heavy cream and the remaining 2 tablespoons of sugar. Using an electric hand mixer, whisk the cream and sugar on high until stiff peaks begin to form.

6. Just before serving the chocolate mousse, top each dish with whipped cream and garnish with chocolate shavings.

RINGARDE RASPBERRY TART

· · · · ● ● ● ♥ ● ● ● · · · ·

Let your ringarde *side run wild with the Ringarde Raspberry Tart. To some, this tart is totally out of style. But to people like Emily, there's something beautiful and fun about celebrating what others overlook. This raspberry delight becomes more pleasant with every bite.*

Makes 6 tarts
· · · · · · · · · · · · · · · · ·

FOR THE PASTRY CREAM

1½ cups whole milk

2 teaspoons vanilla extract

⅓ cup granulated sugar

2 tablespoons cornstarch

4 egg yolks

2 tablespoons butter

FOR THE PASTRY SHELLS

1¼ cups flour

¼ cup granulated sugar

⅛ teaspoon salt

8 tablespoons salted butter, cubed

1 egg yolk

2 tablespoons milk

1 teaspoon vanilla

1 cup fresh raspberries, for topping

1. To make the pastry cream, bring the milk and the vanilla to a boil in a medium saucepan over medium-high heat. Once it has boiled, let it rest for 15 minutes.

2. In a medium bowl, combine the sugar and cornstarch. Whisk in the egg yolks and beat until the mixture is fluffy. Stream the milk mixture into the bowl. Return the mixture to the pot and place over medium-low heat. Continue whisking as the mixture comes to a boil and thickens, about 1 minute, and then turn off the heat. Whisk in the butter 1 tablespoon at a time. Put the pastry cream through a fine mesh sieve so that it flows into a bowl, cover the bowl tightly with plastic wrap, and refrigerate for at least 3 hours.

3. To make the pastry shells, combine the flour, sugar, and salt with the butter in a large mixing bowl. Mix the ingredients together with your fingers until the consistency is crumbly.

4. In a small bowl, whisk together the egg yolk, milk, and vanilla. Add the flour mixture and stir until combined and slightly dry. Using your hands, knead the dough a few times and form the dough into a ball. Wrap the dough in plastic wrap and refrigerate for 15 minutes or so.

5. When the dough has chilled, divide it into 6 sections and form them into small rounds. Use your fingers to gently mold them into mini tart pans and so that the dough adheres to the inside walls of the tart pans. Score the base of each tart with a fork. Refrigerate the molds for 30 minutes.

6. Preheat the oven to 425°F. Line each tart with parchment paper and fill each one with pie weights to secure the molds. Bake for 10 to 12 minutes or until the dough has set. Remove the pie weights and the parchment paper, and then bake for another 4 to 6 minutes, or until the shells are golden brown. Remove from the oven and allow to cool.

7. To assemble, fill the tarts with the pastry cream. Neatly top each tart with a mound of raspberries.

Chapter Five
IT'S APÉRO
Somewhere Cocktails

· · · • • ● ❤ ● • • · · ·

EIFFEL TOWER CHAMPAGNE

· · · · ● ● ● ♥ ● ● ● ● · · ·

It's an Eiffel Tower daydream come true, but this time, there's no one there to sabotage your business dinner. A simple toast to the allure of romance and opportunity, this glass of bubbles is here to remind you that you don't have to be try-hard to have good taste.

Makes 1 cocktail

· · · · · · · · · · · · · · · ·

4 ounces brut rosé

1 strawberry, sliced (and stem removed)

1. Fill a champagne flute with the brut rosé.

2. Garnish with the strawberry slices.

KIR ROYALE

Do as the French do. The Kir Royale is the perfect drink to sip and do nothing,
as they say. Whether yours comes in a can or in a flute is up to you,
but this classic cocktail is all easy drinking and happy days.

Makes 1 cocktail
. . . .

½ ounce crème de cassis

6 ounces champagne

Fresh raspberries

1. In a champagne flute, combine the crème de cassis and the champagne.

2. Garnish with the raspberries.

ALFIE'S SPECIAL MARTINI

· · · · ● ● ● ♥ ● ● ● ● · · ·

When hosting a housewarming party in a new city, one must pay attention to the finer details, and one handsome Brit has a flair for the rare cocktail accoutrements. Cherry and olive skewers? No, thank you! This cocktail is a subtle and tasty play on the martini he makes for himself.

Makes 1 cocktail

· · · · · · · · · · · · · · · ·

2 ounces gin

½ ounce dry vermouth

2 dashes orange bitters

1 olive, for garnish

1. In a cocktail shaker filled with ice, combine the gin, vermouth, and orange bitters.

2. Shake and strain into a martini glass.

3. Garnish with the olive.

LA SEINE SPRITZ

· · · · ● ● ◉ ♥ ◉ ● ● · · · ·

You'll feel like you're sitting by the Seine as you sip this spritz! Enjoy this abundantly cheerful anytime beverage with the same enthusiasm as an ex-pat in Paris.

Makes 1 cocktail

· · · · · · · · · · · · · · · · ·

4 ounces prosecco

2 ounces Aperol

Splash soda water

1 slice orange

1. In a wine glass filled with ice, combine the prosecco and Aperol.

2. Top with a splash of soda water.

3. Garnish with the slice of orange.

EXCLUSIVE LAVENDER MARTINI

· · · · ● ● ● ♥ ● ● ● ● · · ·

Feeling exclusive? Try this luxurious cocktail that turns from blue to an elegant lavender color with a spritz of lemon. Imagine yourself amid rolling lavender fields while you drink this sophisticated concoction. The best part is, it won't smell like a bad batch of perfume.

Makes 1 cocktail

· · · · · · · · · · · · · · · ·

1½ ounces Empress 1908 gin

½ ounce dry vermouth

½ ounce lemon juice

1 sprig lavender

1. In a cocktail shaker filled with ice, combine the gin, vermouth, and lemon juice.

2. Shake and strain into a martini glass.

3. Garnish with the lavender sprig.

SIDE FLING SIDECAR

· · · ● ● ● ♥ ● ● ● · · ·

Get yourself a little love triangle to be oh-so French. If you want to feel the exhilaration of life from the sidecar but perhaps with fewer red flags, choose the liquid version. This classic cocktail is romance in a coupe.

Makes 1 cocktail

· · · · · · · · · · · · · · ·

2 tablespoons sugar

1½ ounces brandy

1 ounce Cointreau

½ ounce lemon juice

1. Line the rim of a coupe glass with sugar.

2. In a cocktail shaker filled with ice, combine the brandy, Cointreau, and lemon juice.

3. Shake and strain into the glass.

TRÈS CHIC FRENCH 75

· · · ● ● ● ♥ ● ● ● · · ·

Get effervescent with the Très Chic French 75. This citrus sipper is bright, bubbly, and feels like a summer day in a glass. Turn that American frown upside-down and do as the French do.

Makes 1 cocktail

· · · · · · · · · · · · · · · ·

1 ounce gin

½ ounce simple syrup

¾ ounce lemon juice

3 ounces champagne

1 lemon twist

1. In a cocktail shaker filled with ice, combine the gin, simple syrup, and lemon juice.

2. Shake and strain into a champagne flute.

3. Top with the champagne and garnish with the lemon twist.

BLACK ROSE

Pick up a bouquet of pink roses from your local floral curmudgeon, but sip on a Black Rose.
This warming cocktail isn't too far from an Old Fashioned but has the sweet flourish
of grenadine to soften the bite of the bourbon.

Makes 1 cocktail
. . . .

2 ounces bourbon

2 dashes bitters

1 dash grenadine

1. In a cocktail glass filled with ice, combine the bourbon, bitters, and grenadine.

BREAKFAST WINE

Drinks before noon? Just follow Mindy's lead and choose a Sancerre. This Breakfast Wine is a light and peppy spritz with gentle citrus and floral attributes. Whether you're keeping other people's secrets or guarding your own like Emily and Cami, this cocktail will be a welcomed reprieve.

Makes 1 cocktail

3½ ounces Sancerre

¼ ounce elderflower liqueur

½ ounce lemon juice

3 ounces soda water

1 slice grapefruit

1. In a wine glass filled with ice, combine the Sancerre, elderflower liqueur, and lemon juice.

2. Top with a splash of soda water.

3. Garnish with the grapefruit.

CHAM-PEAR COCKTAIL

· · · · · ● ● ● ♥ ● ● ● ● · · ·

"Spray it, don't say it!" Actually, you'll want to sip this one. Sit back and smile over this summery cocktail like the best of the Champagne dads out there. With a little luck, you'll keep all your fingers in the process.

Makes 1 cocktail
· · · · · · · · · · · · · · · ·

1 tablespoons cinnamon sugar

2 ounces lemonade

1 teaspoon pear brandy

4 ounces Champagne

1 slice pear, for garnish

1. Line the rim of a cocktail glass with cinnamon sugar.

2. Fill the glass with ice and add the lemonade, brandy, and Champagne.

3. Garnish with the pear slice.

THE TRAVELER

Get your romance and your beverages to go with The Traveler. Emily and Alfie may not have been on their best behavior right before French class, but no one can blame them for making the most of to-go cups. This citrusy shandy is a wink to your favorite Brit and his clever ideas.

Makes 1 cocktail

4 ounces cold lemonade

12 ounces cold light beer

1 slice lemon

1. Put the lemonade in a pint glass.

2. Tilt the glass at a slight angle and pour in the beer.

3. Garnish with lemon.

CHAMBORD SPRITZ

Oui. *This elegantly effervescent drink has its roots in the Loire Valley of France. Sip on this black-raspberry refresher as you hashtag your way through your next adventure.*

Makes 1 cocktail

4 ounces prosecco

1½ ounces Chambord

Splash soda water

Fresh black raspberries

1. In a wine glass filled with ice, combine the prosecco and Chambord.

2. Top with a splash of soda water.

3. Garnish with the black raspberries.

BANKER'S GIN & TONIC

Sometimes you root for a little something London. But whether you are team Gabrielle or team Alfie, this classic cocktail is sure to please with its added sprig of rosemary, unbeatable style, and refreshing honesty.

Makes 1 cocktail

2 ounces London dry gin

4 ounces tonic water

1 sprig rosemary

2 slices lime

1. In a cocktail glass filled with ice, combine the gin and the tonic water.

2. Garnish with the rosemary and lime.

LUXURY OLD FASHIONED

· · · · ● ● ● ❤ ● ● ● · · ·

Belly up to your hot neighbor's bar and indulge in the Luxury Old Fashioned. Just like a certain chef, this cocktail is for anyone who cares about tradition and savors bold flavors.

Makes 1 cocktail
· · · · · · · · · · · · · · · · ·

1 teaspoon sugar

2 dashes Angostura bitters

2 ounces bourbon

1 orange twist

1. In a lowball glass, combine the sugar, bitters, and bourbon.

2. Add ice and garnish with the orange twist.

GRAPEFRUIT MIMOSA

• · · · • • ● ♥ ● • • · · •

A little pamplemousse *for you? Spruce up your mimosa with orange's sprightly sister and toil away your brunch day on a French patio.*

Makes 1 cocktail
· · · · · · · · · · · · · · · · ·
2 ounces grapefruit juice

4 ounces champagne

1 slice grapefruit

1. In a champagne flute, combine the grapefruit juice and the champagne.

2. Garnish with the grapefruit slice.

FRENCH MARTINI

· · · · ● ● ◉ ♥ ◉ ● ● ● · · ·

Never leave your Parisian dream. The French Martini is so coyly delicious that you may want to quit your American job and find out how long you can stick around.

Makes 1 cocktail
· · · · · · · · · · · · · · · ·

1½ ounces vodka

½ ounce Chambord

¾ ounce pineapple juice

1 lemon twist

1. In a cocktail shaker filled with ice, combine the vodka, Chambord, and pineapple juice.

2. Shake and strain into a martini glass.

3. Garnish with the lemon twist.

METRIC CONVERSIONS

If you're accustomed to using metric measurements, use these handy charts to convert the imperial measurements used in this book.

Weight (Dry Ingredients)

1 oz		30 g
4 oz	¼ lb	120 g
8 oz	½ lb	240 g
12 oz	¾ lb	360 g
16 oz	1 lb	480 g
32 oz	2 lb	960 g

Volume (Liquid Ingredients)

½ tsp.		2 ml
1 tsp.		5 ml
1 Tbsp.	½ fl oz	15 ml
2 Tbsp.	1 fl oz	30 ml
¼ cup	2 fl oz	60 ml
⅓ cup	3 fl oz	80 ml
½ cup	4 fl oz	120 ml
⅔ cup	5 fl oz	160 ml
¾ cup	6 fl oz	180 ml
1 cup	8 fl oz	240 ml
1 pt	16 fl oz	480 ml
1 qt	32 fl oz	960 ml

Oven Temperatures

Fahrenheit	Celsius	Gas Mark
225°	110°	¼
250°	120°	½
275°	140°	1
300°	150°	2
325°	160°	3
350°	180°	4
375°	190°	5
400°	200°	6
425°	220°	7
450°	230°	8

Length

¼ in	6 mm
½ in	13 mm
¾ in	19 mm
1 in	25 mm
6 in	15 cm
12 in	30 cm

INDEX